LIFE'S NEW GAME™

Praise for the Authors' Books...

"Whether we admit it out loud or not, we all know there is a level of awareness or understanding about our existence that we're missing out on. There is something else. Our suspicion is that this 'other' level is so powerful that maybe we shouldn't be messing with it. Well don't tell that to Ed Oakley. In Enlightened Leadership in a New Era he's managed to pry open the door to this new world of possibilities just enough for us to peek in. Indeed it will frighten some...but for those of us who want to breakthrough the gravity of our current mindset to the weightlessness of our highest potential this book is a welcomed guide."
Ian Percy, Author of Going Deep and *The Profitable Power of Purpose*

"We use 10% of our brain" ~the Objective, Scientific, Rational, Causative aspect that created all we enjoy today. The other 90% is the Wisdom part: the Subjective, Intuitive, Permitting, Only-Experienced aspect of our brain and life, that few individuals rarely experience. In Enlightened Leadership in a New Era, Ed Oakley masterfully opens wide the door to our Whole Brain and Being to function fully alive in both Objective and Subjective dimensions."
Dr. Ed Carlson, *Founder of Core Health*

"Fear, pain, worry, and conflict have a new place in my life and are serving me now more as tools for growth rather that barriers holding me back from the success that I know is Divinely orchestrated and waiting for me to simply latch on to and move to the next level! Enlightened Leadership in a New Era has really helped me to understand what all of this means and how anyone can breakthrough to influence and significance."
Mark Crowley, *Radio Host and Producer*

"*Enlightened Leadership in a New Era* is a monumentally important contribution to the literature on consciousness and consciousness studies/research. It's also a major advance forward in the conscious/mindful leadership movement. Never before has it been possible for "ordinary people" to have the effect of consciously causing someone to move past the shift point (Threshold of InfluenceTM) on David Hawkin's Map of Consciousness scale.

"Ed has clearly demonstrated this is possible— not only possible, but happening right now!— and that it can happen on a massive scale. I highly recommend *Enlightened Leadership in a New Era* to anyone who is truly interested in advancing their own personal growth, and particularly recommend it to organizational leaders who recognize that leadership of business, non-profits, and governments must change if we are to heal societies and the planet."
Don McCrea, Ph.D.

"*Leadership Made Simple* is excellent! This will be a book read well and often by decision-makers and their teams. I like the examples throughout. It's a winner!"
Nido Qubein, *President, High Point University Chairman, Great Harvest Bread Company*

"In a world where our leaders are overwhelmed with all that needs doing...Enlightened Leadership is a breath of fresh air! The authors deliver on their promise. They provide their audience with a straightforward way of guiding others. Even the busiest of leaders can make time for this."
Beverly Kaye *CEO/Founder: Career Systems International Co-Author: Love 'Em or Lose 'Em: Getting Good People to Stay*

"Just finished the Enlightened Leadership! A great down-to earth approach to leadership. Your examples and simple yet effective processes allowed me to immediately begin solving problems in my head as I read with the Forward Focus. Congratulations!"
Dr. Kevin D. Gazzara *Senior Partner Magna Leadership Solutions*

"You have simply captured the essence of leadership! What I find most impressive about your book is the clarity and simplicity with which complex ideas are put forth – clarity that makes intuitive sense to people without previous training in leadership."
Ariane David, *PhD, National University, Center for Organizational Excellence*

"Leadership Made Simple demystifies what it takes to be a trusted leader but also does it in a simplified way that enables the reader to put the principles into effect immediately and start leading with positive results that provide long-term solutions. Very well done."
Ken Banks *CEO, KAB Marketing Seminole, FL*

"Leadership generally defies description, however the book reminds us that it need not be mystical, or something that one is born to alone. It can be learned, and Making Managers into Leaders is just that, a simple guide to how to learn."
Stuart Ochiltree *Chairman, Universal Life Sciences*

"Effectively balancing the 'hard' with the 'soft' is critical to good leadership. *Leadership Made Simple* provides a practical, results-oriented approach to accomplishing that. The philosophy is proven and effective. I highly recommend it."
Jacqueline Fouse, 2005 *Financial Executive of the Year, Chief Financial Officer, Bunge Limited*

LIFE'S NEW GAME™

Activating the 5 Elements
to BreakOut Success™ in Life & Business

Ed Oakley
CEO Enlightened Leadership

Co-Author of *Enlightened Leadership:*
Getting to the Heart of Change

Liz Hester
IgnitingYOU: 52 Weeks of Inspiration & Action Can
Lead You to Your Dreams

Published in Denver, Colorado, by Enlightened Leadership Publications, wholly owned by Enlightened Leadership Solutions, Inc.

ISBN 978-1-890088-04-0

Contents

Life's New Game Webcast

We know these concepts are complex. In fact, they are often too complex for print, so we've created a webcast where we'll literally break down the complete process and walk you through implementing it in your life step by step. You can join us here: http://lifesnewgame.com/LNGexclusive

INTRODUCTION

This book is written for those people who really want to make a major difference in the world. Many of you already have companies with a vision of doing just that. Many of you are leaders in such companies. Some of you are people who know there is a way you can make a much better contribution to the welfare of the world – *while enjoying life at a higher level yourself.*

This book approaches leadership and exceptional performance differently than you've ever seen and differently than we've ever taught – because only recently have we been blessed with the knowledge and tools to do so. Furthermore, we've never seen these exact approaches anywhere else.

You're a business leader with a vision of how it should all run. You want to make a difference for your customers or clients, and your people. You have a good sense of what that will take. You know your work can help so many people, and you want to optimize just how much difference you can make.

You have considerable frustration that some, if not most of your employees, just don't seem to get it, just don't understand how work could be so much more fun and prosperous for everyone if they would just buy into your vision. They don't seem to understand that there is a direct correlation between having work being effective, fun and prosperous and clients being happy and delighted with your service. You so much want them taking more responsibility for their roles and gaining the gratification of making a much greater difference.

Or, as a small business owner, and a bit of a leader in your industry, you don't understand why you can't break out, why you can't get over the hump of the performance curve and make more of a difference without so much effort. Leverage is what you've been seeking, and you don't know why it's so hard to get there. You so want your team to work well without you, so you can focus on more strategic areas.

For over 27 years, Enlightened Leadership Solutions, Inc. has been helping leaders bring out the best in their organizations in 68 countries, 23 of the Fortune 100 companies, and many governmental, not-for-profit and smaller organizations. While our clients have been well pleased by the measurable results they have attained by working with us – many of the breakthrough results have been astounding! – we have always felt there was even more to true "enlightened leadership" than we yet understood.

Our work has been gratifying and effective, as significant numbers of people on projects and in organizations shifted how they worked with their people. They used our tools like Effective Questions™, Forward Focus™, 5 Action Steps for Breakthrough Results™, Framework for Leadership™, Personal DNA™, Resetting the Zero, Organizational DNA™ and numerous others. When they did that, their people responded and *breakthrough results, higher engagement, happier employees resulted.*

Like *Enlightened Leadership: Getting to the Heart of Change*, a bestseller since its publication over 20 years ago with over 300,000 copies sold, all of our previous books have shared many examples of significant successes for both organizations and individuals. We've always prided ourselves in the simplicity, practicality and effectiveness of our tools, concepts and processes.

1

NEW FRONTIERS

Then, through some life-changing events of our founder, Ed Oakley, we've discovered new frontiers with the:

#1. *Discovery of the clear distinctions in exceptional performers/* leaders that have them stand out that have evaded us – and the rest of the world – for over 27 years.

#2. *The ability to directly, almost miraculously, transfer these distinctive qualities,* not only to individuals, but entire groups of people – as in teams, organizations, groups.

#3. *The ability to teach and transfer these abilities* to you so you can continue your personal/professional development breakout process at your own pace.

This doesn't obsolete what we've been successfully teaching our clients so much as it takes a far simpler approach to automatically support the behaviors that are so important to effective leadership and performance in general. The "how to's" still work exceptionally well. This new work takes the "come from's" to a whole new level.

And we've always said it's not so much what you do but how you do it, or a level deeper, "where you 'come from'" in the process of doing it. Are you coming from trying to use these tools to merely solve the problem? Or just see them as a technique? Or is there a deeper part of you that wants to honor all the parties in the process, to develop deeper relationships among team members, to create an environment that naturally brings out the best in everyone while making a significant contribution to the world? That's a huge difference, and that's a fundamental consciousness issue.

Albert Einstein is credited with saying, "No problem can be solved from the same level of consciousness that created it."

Well, actually, it is more than just a consciousness issue. It is also an issue related to deep emotions we hold, or they hold us, and limiting beliefs that stifle us. So, the concept of where we "come from," which we've discussed with our clients for so many years, turns out to be right on – there's just a deeper level of it that we only now fully understand and know how to address – easily and quickly!

Now we have the ability to directly impact that come-from in you and your people. You no longer have to work at a behavior that is in conflict with your limiting beliefs and emotional experiences. We've been blessed with the ability to facilitate these big shifts in you – in those areas that have limited your effectiveness for many years.

Did you notice we're doing it FOR you? We're both doing the heavy lifting for you and providing you the ability to continue your own development.

The Keys to Getting the Most Out of This Book

- Use it as an opportunity to **look deeply within yourself** for areas you can address more easily than you've ever been able to do before. Take advantage of the opportunity so you don't have to experience the pain I endured to learn this the hard way. *This is an opportunity to greatly leverage your life and your leadership.*

- **Be open to new possibilities** that don't fit your current thinking limitations. We all have limitations in our thinking – based on our backgrounds, upbringing, education, home environment, personal experiences, work experiences, etc. **For those open to it, this work will remove those limitations**. You must be open to seeing things differently. Some of these discoveries have challenged us as well, but now *we've seen the direct results*.

- **Focus in the first part on you as a person and leader**, the more you've developed yourself, the easier this part will be, but remember we can always help you with either part.

- **Focus in the second part on how to bring out the best in your people** and optimize organizational results in ways never seen before.

For over two decades, we've taught concepts of: "Turning on the lights" and "Lightening the load." (Thanks Doug Krug for these awesome concepts.)

"Turning on the lights" was about turning on the lights of awareness of the little things we, as leaders, do and say. And subtle changes in the things we can do and say that bring out the best in those around us. *Now we turn on the lights of awareness directly within!*

"Lightening the load" was about creating an environment in which we can count on the people around us being responsible for their work and allowing us to focus on the job of leadership. *Now we transform our inner and outer environments at the source!*

Everything we taught about that being a significant part of "enlightened leadership" was true then and still is. Having said that, our recent discoveries have put whole new meanings on these terms and new, simple action to put them into practice.

We were always training the leader, wishing we could reach in and change their inner game - where transformation is most effective and lasting...*Now we do!*

Welcome leader to this, your Life's New Game!

"Working with Life's New Game to accelerate the vision of my business has been amazing! From the time we started, things accelerated like a Tesla Roadster on a velvet highway. I have a true awareness of my role and power, and the ability to focus it as never before. This has taken my creativity through-the-roof and my true mission is unfolding before my eyes. My revenues are up as I'd expect them to be. But what's more, I'm having the time of my life! Thanks guys!" M. Gilbert

2

LET THE GAME BEGIN!

Life's New Game was thrust upon me without warning. I didn't ask for it. At the time it began, I certainly didn't want it. And it has been one of the greatest blessings in my life.

I was Living a Great Life!

- I traveled to exotic locations around the world once a year
- I had written a best-selling book and developed leaders in 68 countries through the company I founded, Enlightened Leadership Solutions
- I was speaking and training to great audiences
- I was finding time to travel in my own airplane
- I was enjoying the game of tennis, etc., etc.

Then it happened. What at first was to seem like the greatest tragedy of my adult life, actually led to universal keys to breaking out in life and business – gifts that have been worth all the misery I went through and are already benefiting many others around the world.

I'm eager to share with you the breakthrough realizations I had about bringing out the best in individuals, teams and organizations

– even though I had already been doing that kind of work for over 27 years at a highly recognized global level – I've learned so much more! And now I'm ready to share with you that secret something that less than the top 5% of leaders have, that separate them from all the rest.

Welcome to the Top 5%

Years of experience has taught me that only the top 5% are drawn to this work. The fact that you're reading this likely means you're already close to that level of performance in your work and your life. So welcome to the Top 5% who want to move to the 1%! I trust this work will catapult you well into the ranks of those making the greatest difference in their lives, in their teams and in the world. But first, I must tell you a bit about my personal story that led to this deep understanding of what makes some leaders stand out.

You see, I was overwhelmed with a debilitating rash all over my body – itching horribly day and night, getting very little sleep, and finding it difficult to focus on anything. Suddenly my focus wasn't on business or even relationships. It was on me!

Little did I know that I was being presented with one of the greatest opportunities in my sixty-some years. It sure didn't feel like an opportunity. It felt like something I just wanted to survive, to get through, to get back to life as usual. But, somehow I sensed this was not that simple. I sensed that this was a "wake-up call" – that I had a choice: to deal with this issue head on at it's source, or wither away toward the end of life.

I'm Going to WIN

The decision actually wasn't easy. Part of me just wanted to give up. I remember the night when I made the decision to fight. It was the turning point. I decided I'm going to do what it takes to win this battle. As soon as I made that decision, it seemed I was guided to ideas and resources unknown to me before. It was like the universe had responded to my decision to address this challenge in a powerful way.

Now, I'd like to say that it responded with an easy solution that would have me back to normal life the following week. I'm afraid it wasn't that easy. It was also a test to see how badly I wanted to win this battle.

Resources Came Out of Nowhere

I was miraculously guided to Dr. Ed Carlson's Heart Forgiveness and Core Health work (see Appendix). Through that work, I realized that what was "killing" me were deep, debilitating emotions that were stored throughout my body. It started with Anger and went from there, even though I felt I'd cleared that – a number of times in my life! I was trusting what I was reading, and here he was giving me indications that much Anger was still there and a straightforward way to clear it.

Really? I had dealt with anger and other emotions a number of times – using different approaches and different resources. I didn't feel there was significant anger left. Likely you feel the same. Yet everything I read and felt suggested it was still there, and deep down, I knew it was. So, I launched into Dr. Carlson's guided visualizations to deal with the first big anger, anger with others. Just a few hours later, the process was complete.

There was a New Peacefulness

Surprisingly, and thankfully, I felt different. There was a distinct difference, a peacefulness that was new – that I had never experienced before. If I hadn't noticed a clear difference, I probably wouldn't have continued, but I felt a difference, so I vowed to continue!

I was shocked to realize how straightforward the process was. After a few weeks of clearing these emotional issues every chance I could, I felt distinctly better, and the rash was not as constantly debilitating. I was even sleeping better.

I soon found myself at a Friday night conference when my ophthalmologist friend, Dr. Bill Hines, stood up and told of his experience of being "awakened," and the impact it had on his life. He told of recently being in a surgical situation, after the "awakening," that was not going well. Things got very complicated very fast, and he didn't know what to do. Suddenly, in that emergency, everything became very clear, and he started taking action that he had never done before. He felt completely guided by an outside force. It was a miracle.

When he finished speaking, I cornered him. I wanted to know more. I discovered there was a week-long process he experienced, and it was available to me too. I thought, "You know, I've endured so much pain and done so much work on myself, I'm going to do this as a gift to myself. I'm not sure what this "awakening" thing is, but it can't hurt me."

Knowing that the course was coming up rapidly, I was also motivated to complete the deep emotional clearing work I was doing – literally finishing on the long flight to the retreat location. So, here I was at my retreat a month later, ready to enjoy it and see how much value I could gain. It was a very good, enjoyable and thought-provoking experience.

Only after the experience as I was reflecting on what happened, I realized there had been a significant shift, what they called "awakening," but wasn't sure what it really was. On a relative scale, I knew how to measure my own degree of insight, focus, motivation, energy, clarity and creativity. The day after returning from the retreat, I was feeling pretty un-focused, un-motivated and I was a little concerned. What have I done to myself, I wondered?

They had suggested there would be a period of integration and by the third day, my energy, motivation, creativity, insight, focus and clarity were MORE than 100% of my norm. The next day, it was even HIGHER, and it kept going up almost daily for a week or so, not just in small increments, but substantial jumps.

I was soooo clear…about decisions…about what's important… about what to do…about what not to do…about moving forward. It was amazing. My mind was so clear! And I knew that feeling – it was that of being in the flow, in the zone, on-a-roll – yet it was lasting for longer periods of time.

- My **energy**? Through the roof!

- **Motivation**? Couldn't remember ever having anywhere near what I had now except for short spurts.

- **Focus**? Like a laser. Amazing.

- **And creativity**? My mind was racing with it. I started journaling to capture insights about every aspect of my life, my business, and moving forward into whole new ventures – like what eventually became Life's New Game.

Six weeks after experiencing the "awakening" retreat, I went to the mountains and wrote a book about my experience *in just five days*. I've written books in five months, but five days is amazing for most anyone!

Spontaneous Healing!

Then, right after the book was finished, at 2:00am on May 27th, 2013, I was spontaneously healed of my debilitating illness, gluten intolerance, an auto-immune disease. Yes! Completely healed though I had been told I'd have to manage it for the rest of my life. A major blood test soon confirmed it was true – the disease was gone!

Two days later I had the most delicious pepperoni and artichoke pizza of my life – one bite at a time as I carefully watched for any issues. No reaction! The next day I had one of my favorite things – a milkshake – milk having been on my "do not eat" list, too. No reaction whatsoever. I have been eating anything and everything I wanted ever since!

Less than half a year after being struck by a life-changing, debilitating illness, I had not only been completely cured of the illness, but I had been given a powerful and important gift – though I wasn't clear about what that gift was early on.

Because of the spontaneous healing of my illness, I first thought that "the healing" was the important part of my experience and learning, and I was eager to write about it. I was soon to learn, however, that there was much more to share than I knew so far. Learning was valuable and important to me, but there was more to this gift than I yet realized, and I was highly motivated to understand it deeper.

Minor Miracles Pile Up

Furthermore, I had a series of what I'll call "minor" miracles that happened since my "awakening" adventure. Here are several examples:

- Coming back from the week-long retreat, I was boarding the plane. When they went to take my ticket, they said, "Mr. Oakley, could you please step over here? **We'd like to offer**

you a complimentary upgrade to our advanced, International Business Class." How often does that happen these days!

- I was riding my bike a lot faster than advisable along the dirt and gravel Highline Canal trail in the South Denver, Colorado area. I reached down with one of my hands to get my water bottle for a drink as I rode. I accidentally dropped the bottle, pushing it out in front of the bike in my attempt to hold onto it. In a flash, I reflexively closed my other hand on the brakes to keep from running over the bottle. Bad move. **The bike stopped. I didn't. I went flying over the handle bars and onto the path in front of the bike.** There was a couple walking behind me who saw it all. They were frightened – just knowing I was badly hurt. I got up off the ground looking all over my body for the injuries. Nothing! **I couldn't find a single scratch or bruise**! They were more shocked than I was. We were all convinced it was a miracle.

- Another time I was riding my bike several miles from our Keystone, Colorado mountain condo when there was a bolt of lightning and an immediate peal of loud thunder. Concerned, I immediately turned around and headed back home. As I reached the River Run village, things had calmed down, so I considered whether to stop for some lunch. With that thought, a single drop of rain hit me in the face. *Without thinking*, I immediately peddled vigorously off to the condo. As I pulled up to the garage, it started raining. By time I was inside, it was a full-blown storm. **I realized how I was guided and how I had heard the guidance each step of the way.** This was new for me. Maybe I had been guided in the past, but it wasn't nearly as clear that I was, or I was not in a place to hear it or realize it.

- Returning from another trip, I arrived back to my Denver

office right about lunchtime from Tampa, Florida. I immediately got to work, and was really feeling productive. I was on-a-roll! I glanced at the computer clock at one point, and it said 4:45pm. Great, I thought! I've gotten a days worth of work done in just four hours! Imagine my surprise when I glanced at the computer clock again, just a few minutes later, and it said 2:49pm. I was shocked. I had to stop to think what was going on. The computer had just now adjusted for Mountain time from the Eastern time it had been on in Tampa. **The work I felt so good about accomplishing in four hours had actually been done in two hours**! I've had numerous such 'time miracles' since.

Because all this had happened so quickly after the retreat, I jumped to the conclusion it was all because of the shift at the retreat. Yet, as my life was soaring, I talked to others who had been at the retreat whose lives were more challenged than ever. What was different about me? Why was I thriving and they weren't...

Something Doesn't Make Sense!

Life was exciting as little miracle after little miracle occurred. My debilitating autoimmune disease was history. The insights I was having were amazing. I hadn't been so motivated in years. I began to contemplate how I could make an even greater difference on the planet with what I was learning. But something wasn't making sense. I began communicating with a number of people who had the same transformational experience, the same course I took. I was excited for us all to share the breakthroughs in our lives.

There was only one problem. *They weren't having the same level of breakthroughs, insights, energy, motivation,* etc., that I was. In fact, some of them were downright struggling with life. At least one seemed really disappointed in the results of their experience in the same class for which I was elated. What was the difference?

Why was my situation so different than theirs? Don't get me wrong. They were having some good moments. But not even close to the consistency of personal and professional breakthroughs I was having.

Then I realized…What had I done BEFORE going to the retreat?

I had cleared a massive amount of deep, limiting or negative emotions through Dr. Carlson's work. Virtually no one else had done that. They came to the retreat with baggage and left the retreat with those emotional issues, surface or deeply buried, that they had before the 'awakening' experience.

If they had issues with anger or worry or jealousy or anxiety or judgment or fear before they were awakened to a new level of awareness, they still had them. *The shift from the retreat did not change those emotional limitations.*

So, what made me different than others at the retreat a few months earlier? The thing that distinguished me over everyone else is that I had cleared a massive amount of deeply ingrained emotions and limiting beliefs before doing the retreat. I now realize it was not just the mindset shift, but the **combination of clearing** debilitating emotions and limiting beliefs and the consciousness shift that made the total difference. I realized I'd been guided to a new understanding about how to enhance human performance.

But wait, you're saying. That was a hell of a lot of work you just described to clear the emotions alone. Stay tuned. There was more to the puzzle than I currently realized, and it got a whole lot easier.

It Took 2 to Tango

I was very excited about these highly unusual, yet powerful experiences I was having. There was just one fly in my ointment. I had no one that fully understood it all and could also help envision how to have the greatest impact on humanity with it. A gap existed… for a short while. But by now, solutions were showing up in my life almost miraculously, so…

It was the opening day of the three-day Experts Industry Association annual meeting. I was a little late joining the other several hundred members in a crowded Marriott hotel ballroom in Santa Clara, California. The place was packed, and there were few seats remaining. Finally, I spotted one down a row about ten seats over. I worked my way over to it with multiple apologies and soon found myself sitting beside a very attractive young woman. Now, what are the odds that the one seat I would find in a packed industry conference would be beside a pretty woman?

That was only the beginning. After chatting briefly during the session, I would occasionally see her around the conference. Every time I did, she would have something interesting and significant to say – as if the universe meant it just for me. Each time it was a little startling – until I learned to expect it.

On the second day, we had lunch together with a half-dozen other people, and I got to know her a little better. I realized she was quite high in consciousness (we'll discuss later), literally brilliant, and understood the things that had been happening to me better than I did. She also had a significant vision of how I might want to take this evolving work into the world for the greatest impact. So, an interesting connection was already made as we departed to our homes in Texas and Colorado.

We Were Blessed!

Her name was Liz Hester and we discovered early on in our frequent video conferences that there was an amazing synergy between the two of us. When she had a significant positive shift, I did, too, and vice versa. We discovered that when we were doing work together, progress was many times faster and more effective than if just one did it – and we were blessed with complementary capabilities and a drive to impact the world.

We also seem to have been given special gifts at the same time. It became clear that we were brought together for a significant purpose, and that is more and more clear every day. A few months after first meeting her, I invited Liz to be my partner in "Life's New Game."

Soon we would come to know the profound nature of the honed skills and gifts given to us, and we would see we could bring them out into the world in ways that could transform the lives of many people and the effectiveness of many organizations. You too are part of that process.

So what did we discover about leaders who change the world and how to create new ones? I think the answer might surprise you.

> *"Working with Ed & Liz has been life-changing. Even though I thought I knew what I was doing spiritually, they gently steered me toward several concepts that I completely missed, and those made all the difference in my peace and understanding. But there's more. Recently I had an issue with unexpected unpaid taxes. Ed helped me with Life's New Game to ground and clarify what was really needed and 30 minutes later, all anxiety was gone. Thank you, for your substantial contribution to the quality of my life."-M.S.A. Smith*

3

OUR MOST PROFOUND MOVERS

How Emotions Affect Us

By now you've spent some years in personal development and business development. You've learned that humans make decisions based on emotions, not facts. Yes, we look at data, but when push comes to shove, we move when we feel like it. Decades of research and training have been devoted to the role emotion plays in decision making.

Now wouldn't it be nice if you had a way to address the emotions that are moving you *directly*...and quickly instead of reacting unconsciously? We're not talking about "managing" anger or "acting happy till you are happy." We're talking about real change directly at the source.

Your Most Limiting Emotion Exposed

Our studies estimate that as much as 85% of the limitations we face due to our emotions is deeply buried Anger. It tends to show up clearly in the behaviors of some people, but not so obviously in others. In fact, you'll remember that I thought I was mostly free of anger, yet there was a heck of a lot lurking under the surface.

Dr. Carlson's *Heart Forgiveness* course suggests there are three levels of anger:

- Anger with Others (Aothers)
- Anger with Self (Aself)
- Anger with God and the World (Agworld)

I'm sure you've experienced people who show their anger easily and lash out at the slightest provocation. I'll bet you know a few who focus their anger on themselves and drive themselves into the ground. Both are highly debilitating, yet now easily curable.

Because anger has so much impact on us, we're going to focus most of the "emotional" content of this book on anger and explore how it limits our performance in life, how it affects our health, etc. That said, nearly everything we discuss about clearing anger applies to other emotions, too – including anxiety, grief, jealousy, worry, various fears, hurt, guilt, etc. The negative emotions we carry are like heavy baggage that weighs us down. These emotions pile up and form a dense fog that blocks our clarity and saps our energy.

Mastering the Anger Scale

Anger is such an impactful emotion, that we have created a scale to measure our anger level and our progress on clearing it. Our Anger Scale (AS) is a general measurement of one's emotional situation, stability or concern. We created the scale made of single digits from 0-10, except when it is close to zero, when we will use less than 0.5 (<0.5) if it is. Also, if we just say AS = x value, we are actually talking about anger with others.

To put this scale in perspective...

Anger Scale (AS)

```
10
9        Hitler
8
7
6
5
4
3
2        Average Person
1
<.5      Mahatma Gandhi
0
```

As you can see, you'd like to be sitting pretty with Gandhi around 1 rather hanging out with Hitler around 9!   Both the average and median AS around the world are approximately AS = 2.

When you clear your anger, all three of them, it is a major accomplishment. It will definitely be a time to celebrate! Our process of clearing your anger can quickly and easily get you to the point of having < 0.5 anger with others, anger with yourself, and anger with God and the world. That's a huge breakthrough for 99.9% of the population.

We have found that many of the best leaders tend to have AS <= 1. That makes sense as we've found that real leadership is so much about influencing others in positive, encouraging ways. Notice we said "tend to."

We were initially confused by finding some people who we consider exceptional leaders who have AS = 2 or 3, and sometimes even 4. "How could that be?" we asked. Our research had continued for months with some astonishing results but something was bothering us about focusing solely on anger. Finding exceptional leaders with a higher AS supported our feeling that we were leaving something out. It was time to look at all emotions as a whole.

The key is balance.

Finding the Balance

Now it all made sense. We had focused so much on the 'heavy' emotions, since they cause us the greatest pain, but in life there must be balance – a yin to a yang. We'd been clearing the 'heavy' or 'negative' emotions. But we had been ignoring the 'light' or 'positive' or Forward Focused emotions.

The major strengthening emotion we had not been considering is Love, or caring. Love might even be seen as the counterpart of anger. If Anger is on one side of the seesaw, Love hangs out on the other.

If caring or love is strong enough, it balances anger to a significant extent. "Love conquers all" has a lot of truth in it. Caring for our fellow human beings can override our buried anger if the anger is not too strong and the caring is strong enough.

As we looked at excellent leaders with Anger Scale of 2 or 3, in every single case they had a very high Caring Scale. Just like anger, we see caring/love as having three components:

- Caring for Others (Cothers)
- Caring for Self (Cself)
- Caring for God and the World (Cgworld)

Mastering the Caring Scale

Love is such a powerful emotion, that it also gets its own scale to measure our progress on strengthening Caring. Our Caring Scale (CS) as a general measurement of one's general caring of others, self and world. We defined the Caring Scale in % up to 100%. When someone measures in the area of 95% or greater on the Caring Scale (CS), it balances out a lot of anger.

To put this scale in perspective…

Caring Scale (CS)

0%
10%   Hitler
20%
30%
40%
50%
60%
70%
80%   Average Person
90%
98%   Mahatma Gandhi
100%

As you can see, you'd like to be at a lovely rally with Gandhi around 98% rather than with Hitler goose stepping around 10%! The average AS around the world is approximately CS = 80%. It is not a linear scale, though, so 90% is much, much higher than 80%.

When you strengthen Caring, all three of them, it is a major accomplishment – Celebrate! When you raise your caring to 95% or higher on Caring for others, Caring for yourself, and Caring for God and the world, you show up very differently. Your leadership ability jumps dramatically. That's another huge breakthrough for 99.9% of the population.

We have found that many of the best leaders tend to have Caring Scale > 95%. That makes sense here too as we've found that real leadership is still so much about influencing others in positive, encouraging ways.

How They Balance

What is fascinating is that if your love of others is very high, say 98%, you can actually have higher anger of others, e.g. AS = 3, and you can still be an excellent leader and high performer. Caring is stronger than anger, and that's empowering to know.

Up to this point, all my clearing of emotions had been through the utilization of the powerful processes taught by Dr. Carlson. The only way I could help anyone else clear their emotions was to recommend his workbook and CD's and take several months or more to utilize the guided visualizations to clear their own emotions.

The process was valuable, but long, and few had the physical disability I had at that time to drive them to keep clearing till they were completely healed. This was a severe frustration for me, because I knew the value it would bring people. It was powerful for me, and I knew it would be powerful for others. There had to be an easier, faster way to bring this to others.

My Higher Self Steps In

On December 21, 2013, I met a young woman at a get-together. This time, she found me, because a friend had told her of the incredible results I was having in doing emotional clearing and raising awareness.

It quickly became apparent to me that Edith had some serious anger issues. I felt the energy radiate from her and I could better understand and empathize when I heard later that she had lost her child. I knew Dr. Carlson's work could help her, but I had no confidence she would be willing to follow through with the work from where she was in her life just then. So, I comforted and supported her as best I could.

I went home frustrated that I couldn't help her in an easier way. As I sat in bed, I closed my eyes and fervently prayed for a way to help her more directly. I prayed with all the pent up energy of my frustration for several minutes – pretty much begging for a way to help people like Edith. Surprisingly, I got an answer through a very clear insight.

The insight was that I could just ask my Higher Self to work with her Higher Self to clear what was needed. This came to me so intuitively and easily that I wasn't quite sure if it was real, but it felt very powerful, so I decided to test it.

I went through a measurement process for Edith as if we were doing Dr. Carlson's Heart Forgiveness process from the beginning. Once I did the measurements, I had a sense of how long the clearing process might take if it worked at all. I decided to try the process for just ten minutes, not long enough to clear all of her anger with others, but long enough to diminish it significantly, then re-measure to see if anything had changed.

I gave the process my best shot. I paused and tested after ten minutes, and wow, based on the measurement, it seemed to work! The anger with others level had dropped significantly. Not quite believing it, I decided to see if it remained at that lower level all night. After my sleep, repeating the test revealed the process had indeed lowered the level of anger with others for Edith and remained at that lower level. I was so excited! Now to determine if this is real or just my imagination.

I got in touch with Edith the next day and told her about my experience and asked if she was open to experimenting with releasing her anger – with no expectations, of course. She was all for it, so I set out to clear all of her anger with others and anger with herself over the next couple of days. I did the work, then texted her to let her know and to encourage her to watch for changes. Several days passed by and I pretty much forgot about it.

Then I got an extensive text from Edith. She said that things at work had changed for the better. She was enjoying being there. She was now enjoying one of the employees that she previously had issues with. She felt very different and was most grateful for my help.

I had been blessed with the ability to facilitate the clearing of another person's emotions! I was filled with gratitude, and I was quite clear I wasn't doing the work. I was just asking their spiritual team to support them in clearing the emotions that were currently an issue. Now I could bring this work to more people, knowing that there is a powerful, easier and faster solution to their pain…and their joy!

My greatest personal interest is in helping develop leaders and their teams in organizations to greatly enhance the effectiveness of the organizations through enhancing the lives of the people. It was time to see if I could take this technology to groups for a more leveraged impact on the world.

So, on Christmas Day, I experimented by clearing anger with others for my three children, my daughter-in-law, my son-in-law and my niece all at the same time. In fact three of them, including my niece were not even present. A few hours after the process, my sister called me from Virginia saying how whatever I had done had made a big and very positive difference in my niece and her actions. They both were ecstatic – thinking I was a miracle worker.

The experiment worked, thus demonstrating our ability to impact groups and organizations at the same time. This opened the door for bringing Life's New Game to whole organizations. We would soon verify this by working with a couple of entire organizations. That's the leveraged effect on the world we wanted!

Before we dive into the exact method we used for this individual and mass transformation, we'd like to introduce you to the tool we use to measure the change. This tool has been foundational to our work and verified through the stories and results of our clients. It's much more scientific and simple than you'd expect if you've never used it ;)

4

HOW DO WE MAKE ALL THOSE COOL MEASUREMENTS?

We love sharing our measurement methodology, and it's a question we might ask you, too! After all, how do you measure anger and love? It's not like you can cut them out and put them on a scale. Fortunately, science has given us a handy tool called applied kinesiology.

While this might be a new, even challenging idea to some, we've actually been studying and demonstrating the basics of this capability during our various Enlightened Leadership workshops and seminars for many years.

We first started using this technique after reading Dr. David Hawkins extensive research in *Power vs Force.* Dr. Hawkins built on the initial of work of Dr. George Goodheart, who pioneered the specialty and also leans significantly on the work of Dr. John Diamond, MD, who refined the specialty into what he called behavioral kinesiology in 1979 in his book, *Your Body Doesn't Lie.*

While health practitioners and nutritionists use this technology extensively to discover health issues with the body, we have found that the same methodology has been very handy in measuring 'truth' vs 'fiction,' 'true' or 'false,' 'yes' or 'no.'

In our workshops, we use the arm test, or muscle testing, which Dr. Hawkins recommends. We'll have a big, strong guy come to the front of the room, and have him hold out his arm parallel to the floor. We'll say "be strong" and press lightly on his arm. The arm won't move much because it is strong. It will be solid. A "true" indication. We'll then have him state his name and hold strong. The arm will be strong because he is truly the name he said.

Then, we'll have him say something obviously false, like "my name is Susan." His arm will be easy to press down as it is weak. A "false" indication. His statement was false. It always shocks the big, strong man when he cannot maintain his strength while "lying." That's pretty clear, so we go to the next level.

We'll have him turn around away from the class, and give silent instructions to the class to send him silent but negative thoughts. We'll test his arm while that's going on, after asking him to be strong, and it will be weak – no matter how hard he tries to be strong. We have him state what he experienced. He knew it was weak. This gives you some idea of the impact of negative thoughts from people around you. The good news is that we don't have to be at the mercy of negative thoughts, and we demonstrate that in the class, as well.

That method works great…if you have someone handy 24/7 to push on your arm. Because I didn't have an 'arm pushing assistant' when I was doing massive amounts of Ed Carlson's emotional clearings, I had to become very proficient at using a pendulum for the same purpose. The pendulum is used to test "yes" or "no" based on the direction it moves. The trick, or the breakthrough, you have to accomplish is not letting your conscious mind influence the outcome. That's not easy for everyone, which is why we offer some of our testing services.

Where Truth is Known

What you are seeking are answers from your unconscious mind, which is far more powerful than your conscious mind. What's more, your unconscious mind is constantly connected to the Higher Consciousness. *It's like having access to the universal data base of information.* The idea is that your body and muscles are closely aligned with your Higher Self or Universal Energy, where all truth is known.

Your body muscles are directly connected to your Higher Self and therefore the Higher Consciousness. Using muscle testing allows you to get answers from your body without your conscious mind intercepting the signal and changing your answer. Therefore, this approach provides access to knowledge of truth or fiction, yes or no, true or false.

For more information on how to master muscle testing with a partner, or the pendulum for yourself, see references in the Appendix. It's important to your clearing work if you're going to do it on your own, but far beyond the scope of this book to teach you how to do it. We do spend some time teaching the technology in our classes.

My Painful Route to Mastery

I think a few words about how I came to be proficient in using the pendulum effectively might be useful. The year 2013 was one of the toughest years of my life. Very early I acquired a massive rash all over my body, to which I've referred several times earlier in the book. The itching was so bad at times, I would break down in tears. I could hardly wear clothes at the worst times because of the sensitivity of my skin. Even bed sheets irritated my skin. I was sleeping typically 4 to 5 hours per night at the most.

When numerous doctors couldn't figure out the cause and only wanted to deal with the symptoms – namely cortisone shots to relieve the symptoms, I somehow knew that would be a mistake. If I removed the symptoms, I'd never deal with the real issues. At 64 years old, I saw this as the biggest wake-up call I'd ever received. I somehow felt there were important lessons for me to learn – deep issues to clear, even though I had done different modalities of therapy and healing work for many years.

Some of the most important healing processes I used were Dr. Ed Carlson's courses, for which Energy Measurement, his brand of advanced kinesiology, was needed. While I had been dabbling with muscle testing for years, I got very, very serious about it at this time – using it every day many times – getting better and better all the time. I knew I had become very good with it when my friends and family started coming to me to ask me to do some tests for them with my pendulum. :-)

Is this all a load of bunk? Can your body really tell you what is true or false?

There are a number of 100-hour Applied Kinesiology certification courses available from Los Angeles to New York City, aimed at professional health care providers. I honor them and have no doubt that these professionals know far more about this than I do. But you don't need certification to use it effectively.

There are arguments on both sides, though the serious certifications add credibility in my mind. Also, we have found remarkable progress in our personal and professional lives from utilizing Energy Measurement as one of our key tools – for decision-making, clearing emotions and measuring effectiveness of our planning and efforts.

Leaders who work with us are used to pushing their envelopes of understanding and beliefs and achieving BreakOut Results as a dividend. You can find their results on our website and in this book. If you have read this far, you likely have an open mind and are ready to grow exponentially.

Here's what you can count on. Our results are predictable, repeatable and universal. If I state a calibration or number determined by my Energy Measurement, you can be assured that I have tested that number in at least two ways, and more if I see how to do it. I won't state a result if it is not consistently derived over and over again.

My pendulum is almost always sharp and clear – except when I'm not sharp and clear. I've learned not to even try using it in those situations. Occasionally, something has caused the pendulum to give reverse indications. Actually, it's not the pendulum, it's my issue when that happens. I've learned how to clear myself in those instances. It takes about 30 minutes before I'm ready to use the pendulum again. Or if I'm tired, I just might need to rest. If I do any testing in this environment, I come back and retest when I'm refreshed.

However, if you are feeling your 'BS' button going off, then this work might not be for you at this time. Our methods of measuring are integral to our work and your progress. You can certainly see results without testing, but you will feel much better about your progress and move faster being able to tune to the truth and use benchmarks along the way.

"If this is real, prove it."

I had a conference call with Jeff, the grown son of a business client. I had been working with him remotely, and now was time for a major shift, so I wanted to talk him through the process. He was in Shanghai, China, so I called him on Skype.

His Mom had warned me he was skeptical, but I wasn't prepared for the extent of his doubt. As soon as we got on the call, he said he questioned all these measurements I was making. He wanted me to prove it was real.

"If you can really do this, tell me the color of the piece of paper I'm holding up right now," he challenged. I didn't want to get caught up in a game around measurement, so I said as much. Measuring isn't a parlour trick after all, its a tool. Instead, we went forward with our conversation.

When we finished the mindset-shifting process and hung up, I found myself a bit bothered that I had been afraid to answer his question. Did I really trust my own tools?

So, I wrote down as many major colors as I could think of, which were about a dozen. I took the pendulum and said, "The color of the paper Brandon was holding was…" and I'd name a color. Then the pendulum test would say yes or no.

It said "no" for every color except yellow. I retested and got the same thing. So, I sent off an email to Jeff that just said nothing but, "yellow :-)." About ten minutes later, I got an email from him that simply said, "Nailed it! :-)."

That was validating! But what I nailed wasn't just a color or a skeptic's belief. I nailed the mastery of my tool and the 100% belief and confidence in it. Did it work even when I was in doubt? Yes it did! Jeff himself confirmed it. This tool is so powerful it works whether you doubt or not, so it is worth the time to get the hang of it.

Fine Tuning with the Effectiveness Quotient

Energy Measurement, as described by Dr. Ed Carlson, is the heart of our measurement approach. To make it even more effective, we like to take away the limitations of just true-false, yes-no, positive-negative.

To do that we created what we call Effectiveness Quotient. This quotient is from 0-100%. So instead of counting on a perfect true or false, we are looking for degree of truth from 0 - 100%. This also lets us compare ideas, the effectiveness of our content, really the effectiveness of anything as compared to other options.

Here is a simple example of this in action. We will be publishing this book in a hard format, as well as an ebook format. Given all the parameters and factors involved (cost, presentation, difficulty, time to market, and other things I don't even know), which would be most effective for us to publish, hard cover or soft cover, at this time?

Then I measured:

Effectiveness Quotient for hardcover = 95%

EQ for softcover = 100%

EQ for OTHER = 90%

In this kind of measurement, I always include OTHER because there might be something better I had not considered. If OTHER is 100%, I know I need to think more about the options.

In this case softcover wins out 100% to 95%. Now that might not seem like that much difference, but this happens to be a logarithmic scale, so there is actually a *lot* of difference. Now that softcover has won the test, it might be useful to rationalize all the reasons you can think of for going that way. There are lots of reasons, so I'm comfortable with that decision – at this time. We don't suggest you do that brainstorming before measuring, as you could potentially influence the measurement.

Learning not to influence the measurement is the greatest challenge in Energy Measurement. We find that using the Effectiveness Quotient takes away much of that challenge, because you aren't just looking at yes or no, but at a relative scale.

In the next chapter we'll look at how I used this tool to reveal what seemed like a fatal flaw in my work to that time. After all, if you've identified the change agent, shouldn't it work for everyone? But that did not seem the case and my handy pendulum helped me hone in on the answer.

5

JUST WHAT HAPPENED AT THAT RETREAT?

You'll remember that I experienced quite a shift at the retreat, but I wasn't sure what it was, nor how to quantify it. As I boarded the Lufthansa flight heading home, I was running on questions like, "What just happened to me?" and "How can it be explained more scientifically?" and "What do I already know that somehow ties to this?" and "How can I explain this to business associates without using this odd 'awakened' terminology?"

Once the wheels left the tarmac, I turned on some soft music and lost myself in the quiet world of Mozart. I pulled out my notebook dedicated to this project and started thinking.
While the retreat instructors had talked about raising consciousness of the entire planet, they never really tied "awakening" to consciousness. Was there a direct relationship?

I thought of Dr. Hawkin's book, which introduced his Map of Consciousness, but I'd never been able to measure levels of consciousness (LOC) using his logarithmic model. I wondered if what happened at the retreat would allow me to now? The instructors said there was literally a neuro-biological change in our brains in the process of awakening.

So, what the heck. I got to work to see if I could do this now. I had tried to test my LOC before and got huge numbers – like up close to the 1,000 of Christ Consciousness, so I had a pretty clear hint THAT was wrong. What would I get now? Hmmm. About 615. Is that real? Not sure, but it sure seems more likely to be accurate than 900+ :-)

Who else could I test? Of course! Other people in the class who had "graduated, "i.e., been declared "awakened." I listed some people I had met. I tested the pendulum to see what I got for their Level of Consciousness and I was getting numbers like 612, 618, 621, 608. Very interesting. A clear trend, but how could I know what it meant?

I then asked, "Are these accurate?" and got a very clear YES! Cool! That's a first for my measurement of Level of Consciousness. (See Appendix for detailed measurements of Awakening With and Without Clearing Emotions/Beliefs.)

I needed comparisons, though. So, I thought of friends back home who I considered high consciousness, but who had not been through the same retreat. I picked some of my friends back in Denver who were long-term meditation students and a few others. I wrote down about ten of them who I felt were highly conscious.

I started measuring the first person. 599. Interesting.

The second person: 597. Really!

The third person: 595.

The fourth person: Want to guess the ballpark? You got it, 595 - 599.

All ten had a LOC of between 595 and 599. These are people who had been part of meditation classes, yoga and other personal growth practices for quite a few years, and they were all sitting just below a certain point on the Map of Consciousness! Do you see the accidental discovery?

"Awakening" relates to a consciousness shift to a Level of Consciousness of 600!

I knew that the primary tool of Awakening that I was taught at the retreat was a form of Blessing. So, I should be able to give these Blessings and raise people from wherever they are to above 600, right? My pendulum said "yes" to that, and also that the number of blessings was dependent upon where the person already is in consciousness.

I realized I had an experimental laboratory waiting for me at home. Everyone on my list were all open-minded people. So for now, I didn't need to talk to people about "Awakening." I could discuss with them what happens when they break through the 600 barrier on the Map of Consciousness scale. And speaking about "consciousness" didn't have the same "charge" for me as "Awakening" did.

In his book David Hawkins, MD, introduced his Map of Consciousness as a logarithmic scale from 1-1000, in which he used to discuss the consciousness of people and the characteristics at each level.

Level 1 is barely alive, and the Level 1000 is Christ, Buddha, and Krishna Consciousness. Hawkins estimated that 80% of the people on Earth are actually at 200 or below, which is at a negative, contracting, energy "taking" consciousness level. Hitler, for example, calibrated at 175. Scary, huh?

The subtitle of Dr. Hawkin's book is *The Hidden Determinants of Human Behavior*. Does that get your attention after seeing where

Hitler was? Your level of consciousness is a determinant of behavior – "a," not "the." How many times have you tried to change someone's behavior to no avail. If their consciousness hasn't changed, their behavior is not likely to change either. Consciousness determines behavior to a significant extent.

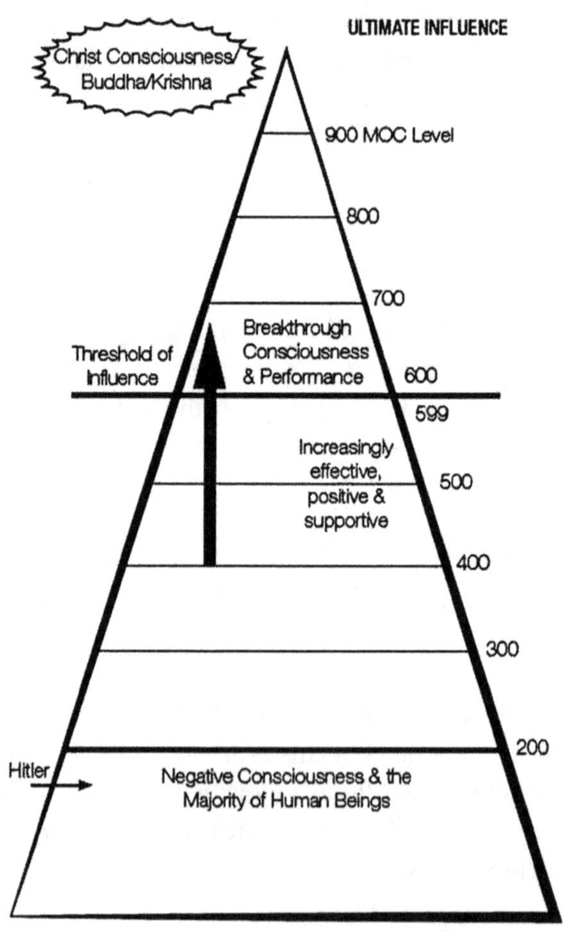

This is very important. Because of the logarithmic nature of the scale, Hawkins estimates that one person calibrating at a consciousness level of 500 offsets the negativity of 750,000 people below 200. Did increasing your consciousness just take a new significance? We hope so!

There are two factors worth mentioning here. Number 1 is that there have been several major positive consciousness shifts on the planet as a whole since Dr. Hawkins first published his numbers. Number 2, you, the people reading this book, would not be anywhere near that low end of the scale, nor would be the majority of people you work with - just because you picked up this book! It is calibrated so that only people of a certain level and above would even read this far – Congratulations!

My measurements suggest this book will most likely appeal to people with LOC (Level of Consciousness) levels of 590 to 750. Frankly, if you've gotten this far, you're probably in that range.

That range is significant because that is where we tend to find so many people who are ready to take the effectiveness of their leadership and their lives to new levels. Because of their consciousness level, they are naturally eager to break through the old limitations. That's also a limited number of people, so this book is not focused on the masses, but more on those people who could most easily and naturally make a bigger contribution to our society through their influence.

When I use the word leadership in this book, *I am specifically talking about the kind of leadership* that contributes to people, work and society, makes a positive difference to people and organizations. They add to our society instead of take away from it and they also are eager to do more.

While I might call them "business leaders," I'm also referring to any kind of leadership, including non-profit, government, or volunteer.

Also note that leadership doesn't necessarily have anything to do with positional authority. An individual with no "authority" at all can, indeed, provide valuable leadership.

Remember, breaking through the 600 LOC barrier raises your influence and effectiveness significantly, and because it is a logarithmic scale, every step above that has you more and more clear, energized, motivated, open to insight, creative and aware.

Imagine that 80% of your current influence is due to your position. That's pretty typical. Now imagine holding the positional influence constant and raising your Personal Influence to the point it is now 80% of your total influence. Now you have some serious influence. That happens naturally with a major consciousness shift AND shift down the Anger Scale AND up the Caring Scale. At the same time your interests are shifting to what is best for all involved. Of course, if you're still reading, you're probably already tending to that way of thinking :-)

Hmmm. Moving down the Anger Scale and up the Caring Scale. That's a lot of work, you might be thinking. Stay tuned. That is no longer true.

In the next chapter, we'll discuss the LOC characteristics of exceptional leaders, as well as their Anger Scale and Caring Scale and how our process allows you to improve simply and exponentially.

> *"I am really blessed and grateful for this opportunity and this class. I have shifted so much, my energy is so much lighter. I am experimenting every day with clearing. I communicate more than hold things in. So I'm very grateful. I appreciate you two. Thank you so much."* Esther

6

3 MINDSET FACTORS OF HIGH PERFORMANCE AND EFFECTIVE LEADERSHIP

"DOING what successful people do is not sufficient;
BEING who they are is the key."
Ed Oakley

It is likely you are reading this book to learn to be a more effective leader as well as a more balanced person. What we found in our research for LNG is that there is a combination of 3 fundamental shifts of mindset that must occur to bring out the very best in yourself, as well as others through your leadership.

Each of these areas by themselves used to take a *lifetime* to become competent, let alone master, but that is no longer the case. Recent breakthroughs, built on decades of proven techniques and success, have vastly shortened the mastery curve. That is exactly why we are writing this book, so you will know what you need to do to optimize your effectiveness in life now and the simple steps to do it.

Can you be an effective leader and angry, hateful and have low self-awareness? Yes, but not the kind of leader for which this book is written. Hitler was very high anger and left an indelible mark on the world. We are writing to and helping enable leaders who leave a positive impression on the world! You are such and the following findings are to help you leave your mark.

Mindset Factor #1: Low Anger

Not surprisingly, the most effective leaders are the least angry. We're not talking anger management here. After all, managed anger is still anger, and the energy lurks just under the surface and tends to leak through into everything you do. We are talking about the actual removal of anger from the system.

Anger Scale <=1 Ideal

For the highest performance individually and as a leader, we find your Anger Scale should be <=2 (assuming a very high Caring Scale.) If the CS score is not so high, an AS of <=1 is required.

Looking at Some Highly Respected, World Changing People

We've taken some highly respected people and leaders of current times and recent past to give you an idea of what a positive, world changing, high performer looks like. These are people we highly respect for who they are and what they do or did. I encourage you to not get caught up in all the numeric data so much as the analysis at the end of the list. The trends are the key.

	Anger Scale
Sir Richard Branson, Billionaire founder of Virgin Group	2
Tony Hseih, Founder, Zappos, author	0.5
Mary Barra, CEO, General Motors	1
Ursula Burns, CEO, Xerox. First African-American woman to head a Fortune 500 Company	1
Anthony Robbins, personal & business development pioneer	2
Marshall Goldsmith, author, *What Got You Here Won't Get You There*	< 0.5
Verne Harnish, author, *Rockefeller Habits* founder, Entrepreneur's Organization	1
Mahatma Gandhi, Leader of Indian nationalism	<0.5
Mother Theresa, Founder, Missionaries of Charity	<0.5

You don't have to have Mother Theresa or Gandhi's low level of anger to make an impact, but being 2 or below makes a big difference to your effectiveness. Interestingly, everyone on this list reduced their Anger Scale numbers, therefore their overall emotional limitations, before experiencing their breakthrough success.

In contrast, we've seen other influential leaders with high anger who have left another kind of mark on the world.

	Anger Scale
Head of major Eastern European country Who has lost world credibility	5
Popular "negative" radio talk show host	6
Head of small, but powerful country in Middle East	5
TV host/ political commentator	6
Mastermind of huge Ponzi scheme, now in jail	6
Average inmate in U.S. prisons sentenced for 20 years or more	7

Likes these people, your level of anger not only influences your performance, but the impact that performance will have on the world.

Have you ever been so mad you felt steam blowing out your ears AND happy? Not likely. Lowering anger makes you happier and the people around you happier too. After all, who from the above group would you like to have over for a dinner party?

We use Anger here for our example, but the numbers are similar for all "negative" or "heavy" emotions, like worry, fear, jealousy, hatred, grief, hurt, anxiety, etc., and our one process addresses them all.

Anger and the negative emotions are not the only factors, though they are often the ones that are the most visible, both in how you feel and to the world. The other 2 factors are critically important to your high performance as well.

Mindset Factor #2: High Caring

We find that the leaders who actually care about others have a much higher performance from themselves and their team…go figure! Balancing caring for others and caring for self is also key. Caring too much more for others, than for self leads to an imbalance than is harmful to the giver. Caring too much more for self than others leads to an imbalance that harms others. Caring that puts others needs first must be balanced with loving yourself in healthy harmony.

Caring/Love Scale >95% Ideal

For optimum effectiveness, we'd like to see your Caring Scale at CS for others = 95% or greater and CS self near 100%, as well. At those levels, your Anger Scale is fine at 2, though we'll be inviting you to get it down well below 1 – you'll thank us for it :)

Let's revisit that list of positive, world changers…(don't worry, we'll put it all together for you at the end and show you what they look like when you put all the factors together.)

	Caring Scale	
	(for others)	*(for self)*
Sir Richard Branson	97%	98%
Tony Hseih	100%	99%
Mary Barra	99%	100%
Ursula Burns	100%	100%
Anthony Robbins	99%	100%
Marshall Goldsmith	100%	100%
Verne Harnish	98%	99%
Mahatma Gandhi	100%	100%
Mother Theresa	100%	100%

The caring numbers are as high as you would expect from this group that has invested so much into making a difference in the world. We would say that love begets love and likely they feel happier and more at home in the world as a nice side effect of all that love.

Some of these had high caring for others in a time that not all returned that love. But they were surrounded by those who did love them and supported them in caring for the world and others. Their level of caring led to a style of leadership that fostered the caring of their team and allowed them to go out and make a significant impact together.

Let's contrast this with that list of less desirable dinner guests…

Caring Scale

	(for others)	*(for self)*
Head of major Eastern European country Who has lost world credibility	81%	99%
Popular "negative" radio talk show host	71%	100%
Head of small, but powerful country in Middle East	80%	100%
TV host/ political commentator	76%	98%

While caring for others offsets a higher of level of anger for the first group, this group is consistently low on that scale, so the anger would not be offset. Their anger would likely be obvious in their behaviors. It is certainly obvious with whom they surround themselves and their effect on the world.

"By their fruits you shall know them." Anger and caring certainly show up in our actions and how we show up in the world. They might have even been painfully obvious to you as 2 of the 3 vital factors in high performance. The third factor is not quite so obvious, and until recently, was not so easy to track.

Mindset Factor #3: High Level of Consciousness

We introduced you to the concept of your Level of Consciousness playing a key role in your effectiveness as a leader, but how high do you have to be?

LOC >700 Ideal

As a minimum, your Level of Consciousness should be above the awakening threshold of 600. Until a couple of years ago, getting to 600 took some major therapy/meditation work, but with the capabilities available today, there is every probability you are already at or over 600. And with our current process, there is no reason you shouldn't get well above 800 quickly, then continue to raise it gradually.

What's the LOC of our list of leaders and world changers?

	LOC
Sir Richard Branson	hi 700's
*Tony Hseih	hi 800's
Mary Barra	800's
*Ursula Burns	800's
Anthony Robbins	hi 800s
*Marshall Goldsmith	hi 900's
Verne Harnish	hi 700's
*Mahatma Gandhi	900's
*Mother Theresa	hi 900's

*indicates above 600 LoC at birth

You can see that they are all above 700, but digging a little deeper, we found something very interesting. Nearly 75% of the master list (below) were born at LOC between 590 and 599. Their consciousness shift above 600 then preceded their world class breakthroughs. Please be clear. Many if not most were "successful" before that consciousness breakthrough – just not world class.

In our other list of negative world changers, they were ALL in the 700s. Seems impossible? High consciousness alone does not mandate positive effect. It is the combination of consciousness, caring and low anger that makes for top performance.

Putting the 3 Mindset Factors Together

Let's put some perspective around the opportunity we all have through lowering our Anger Scale, raising our Caring Scale and raising our consciousness.

We're going to put together the 3 factors together for the lists from before, but first we want to share a big picture scenario that we ran across recently comparing two ends of a spectrum – extreme wealth and poverty.

I'd like to compare our Mindset Factors (LOC, AS, CS) for people who have a net worth of $1 billion or more compared to those who are on some kind of welfare aid in the United States. I know that's an extreme, and I think it is useful to take a look at both ends in contrast.

We're not suggesting that being a billionaire is necessarily something to strive for, or that it is some kind of epitome of success. Nor are we equating welfare to worth, so much as just seeing some value in analyzing the extremes between them and those on the other end of the wealth scale.

Forbes says there are 492 billionaires in the U.S. in 2014.

Those billionaires in the U.S. have the following average Mindset Factors:

	LOC	AS	CS
Billionaires	815	2	95%

Meanwhile, Google reports 108,592,000 people in the U.S. received some kind of government support or aid in the 4th quarter of 2011 (latest data available). Their average Mindset Factors:

	LOC	AS	CS
Welfare	498	5	62%

That's a big picture analysis of one level of monetary success at an extreme vs poverty on the other. The contrast is interesting.

This certainly doesn't mean you'll be a billionaire if you raise your consciousness to 815, lower your Anger Scale to 2 and raise your Caring Scale to 95%. It does say that you are likely to be considerably more successful if you're coming from high awareness, low anger and high caring. And of course, money is only one measure of success. Let's be clear that the average billionaire is successful partially because they are very high on the consciousness scale, average on the Anger Scale, and very high on the Caring Scale. There are certainly other factors involved.

At the other extreme in the U.S., depicted by those receiving some kind of welfare aid, are those people who were far under the "awakening" LOC of 600 at 498. They averaged quite high on the Anger Scale at level 5, and their Caring Scale level of 62% was not nearly high enough to offset the emotional issues suggested by the AS level.

We are talking averages, so we are well aware that there are very wealthy people that don't fit these numbers. However, if they aren't coming from high awareness, low anger and high caring, I'd bet money that they are not likely happy no matter how much money they have.

There are also successful people who are successful monetarily in spite of their consciousness, anger and caring levels. The probability of this happening, however, is very low. And today, these attributes can be easily improved.

So let's put the 3 factors together for our positive, world changers…

	LOC	*Anger Scale*	*Caring Scale*
Sir Richard Branson	hi 700's	2	97% Billionaire founder of Virgin Group
Sara Blakely	hi 700's	1	96% Billionaire founder of Spanx
*Tony Hseih	hi 800's	0.5	100% Founder, Zappos, author
Mary Barra	800's	1	99% CEO, General Motors
Warren Buffet	hi 800's	1	100% Billionaire Chairman, Berkshire Hathaway

	LOC	*Anger Scale*	*Caring Scale*
*Ursula Burns	800's	1	100% CEO, Xerox. First African-American woman to head a Fortune 500 Company
*Malcolm Gladwell	hi 700's	1	98% Best-selling author, journalist, researcher. *The Tipping Point, Outliers, David & Goliath, Blink*
*Marshall Goldsmith	hi 900's	< 0.5	author, *What Got You Here Won't Get You There*, executive coach
Anthony Robbins	hi 800s	2	99% personal & business development pioneer & coach
Wayne Dyer	hi 800's	1	99% speaker, author, *I Can See Clearly Now*
Deepak Chopra	900's	1	00% author, *The Seven Spiritual Laws of Success*
*14th Dalai Lama	hi 900's	<0.5	100% Spiritual Teacher, Leader
Dr. Paolo Macchiarini	hi 800's	<0.5	100% Internationally known surgeon

	LOC	Anger Scale	Caring Scale
*Pope Francis	900's	<0.5	100% Head of Catholic Church
Bill Gates	hi 800's	<0.5	100% Billionaire founder of Microsoft
Verne Harnish	hi 700's	1	98% Author, *Rockefeller Habits*, Entrepreneur's Organization
Ken Blanchard	hi 700's	1	99% Best-selling author, speaker, *The One Minute Manager*, others
Stephen Covey	800's	<0.5	100% Author, *7 Habits of Highly Effective People*
*John Wooden	900's	1	100% UCLA basketball coach, author
Martin Luther King, Jr.	800's	2	98% Civil rights activist, pastor
Rosa Parks	700's	1	96% Civil rights activist, refused to give her bus seat to white person
Nelson Mandela	hi 900's	1	99% President, South Africa
Winnie Mandela	hi 900's	1	100% Activist, First Lady South Africa

	LOC	*Anger Scale*	*Caring Scale*	
*Mahatma Gandhi	900's	<0.5	100%	Leader of Indian nationalism
*Indira Gandhi	900's	1	100	Prime Minister of India
*Mother Theresa	hi 900's	<0.5	100%	Founder, Missionaries of Charity
Eleanor Roosevelt	700's	2	99%	First lady of U.S., but also called First Lady of the World for human rights achievements
Jackie Kennedy Onassis	hi 800's	1	97%	US First Lady, contribution to arts

*indicates above 600 LOC at birth

There are some trends in the people above worth noting:

1. NONE of them had their breakthrough/worldclass successes until they were above the "awakening" Level of Consciousness of 600. Only the ones with asterisks were above the 600 level at birth.

2. Nearly 75% of the list were born at LOC between 590 and 599. Their consciousness shift above 600 then preceded their world class breakthroughs. Please be clear. Many if not most were "successful" before that consciousness breakthrough – just not world class.

3. Furthermore, every one of them reduced their Anger Scale numbers, therefore their overall emotional limitations, before their breakthrough success. Interestingly, all of them were already very high on the Caring Scale early in life. That also can be easily raised, however, perhaps for the first time in our history.

What becomes very clear is that you don't have to be born with ideal Mindset Factors to be a world class success. You can raise your consciousness, lower/eliminate your emotional limitations, and raise your caring for others – thus position yourself for world class success in your area of focus.

So let's look at the negative world changers and see if their factors are consistent with their behavior. When we put all the numbers together, we found an interesting pattern.

	LOC	*AS*	*Caring Scale*	
			(for others)	*(for self)*
Head of major Eastern European country who has lost world credibility	700's	5	81%	99%
Popular "negative" radio talk show host	700's	6	71%	100%
Head of small, but powerful country in Middle East	700's	5	80%	100%
TV host/ political commentator	700's	6	76%	98%

What's different about these people?
The difference lies in their:

1. Level of Anger – These consistently have several times the level of anger as the outstanding leaders we've mentioned above. That leads us to look at the next factor.

2. Level of Caring for Others – They are consistently low on that scale, so their anger levels would not be offset. Their anger would likely be obvious in their behaviours.

3. Level of Caring for Self – They are consistently very high on this scale. This is not an issue when caring for "others" is also very high, but it is the crux of the issue here. When Caring for others is low, and caring for self is very high, egotism and selfishness become characteristic and their negative impact becomes endemic. The high level of anger only increases the power of the negativity in their leadership and in their effect on the world.

Other people with lower consciousness:

	LOC	AS	Caring Scale (for others)	(for self)
Mastermind of huge Ponzi scheme, now in jail	hi 400's	6	51%	99%
Average inmate in U.S. prisons sentenced for 20 years or more	340	7	61%	96%

Interestingly, every single situation in which a professional sports figure has gotten into serious trouble (that we've measured) shows a person with lower consciousness, high anger and low caring for others. The more serious the issue, the lower the consciousness, the higher the anger and the lower the caring for others.

Let's bring this home with some stories closer to the heart...

> *"I just want to reiterate there's a peace about me, that I can only say has come from the course. I feel like I'm not as far advanced and where I want to be, but there's a peace that I will get there and I can accomplish whatever I want."* Norma

7

EXAMPLES FROM THE HEART

In *David and Goliath*, Malcolm Gladwell explores how everyday people making a lasting change in the world. The book had inspired me before and when I picked it up again, I found that Life's New Game had given me a unique perspective on the differences in behavior in the case studies. I would like to tie those differences in one particular set of stories to two factors – where they were on the Anger Scale and the Caring Scale.

The example I've chosen is the comparison between two contrasting responses to the loss of a child by murder. Looking at such a life altering event throws behaviors into sharp relief so we can see them more clearly. I have tremendous empathy for both individuals and honor both of them for their totally different approaches. I have 3 children myself. How would I have responded? Depending on the stage of my life, I could see me responding BOTH ways.

Mike Reynolds

In 1992, Mike Reynolds' 18 year old daughter came home from college to go to a wedding. She was happy and expectant and Mike had the following Mindset Factors:

		LOC	AS	CS
Mike Reynolds	Daughter Home	700's	4	85

While home, she went out with friends. As they were getting into their car, two men accosted them and demanded her purse. She resisted, and one of the men shot her in the head. When Mike came home from the hospital where his daughter had died of a gunshot wound from a man who had been in and out of jail seven times and had just been released again from prison, his Mindset Factors had shifted:

		LOC	AS	CS
Mike Reynolds	Daughter Home	700's	4	85
	Daughter Died	900's	5	85

Certainly not surprising the Anger Scale it would jump up.

Immediately after the death, Mike and the situation got a lot of public attention, including two hours on a radio talk show that got into looking at the criminal justice system limitations. With this kind of "support," Mike went down a path of influencing the changing of California laws and specifically to the "Three Strikes" law, which says on the third conviction, you're in jail for life, even if for minor offenses. That law was radically scaled back in 2012, as it had not accomplished its intention. It certainly left its mark on criminals, yes, but also on innocent victims.

Now let's look at another grieving parent…

Wilma Derksen

In November 1984 Wilma and Cliff Derksen's 13-year-old daughter, Candace, was riding the bus home from school in Winnipeg, Canada, but she never arrived. At the time Wilma Derksen's daughter disappeared, her Mindset Factors were:

		LOC	*AS*	*CS*
Wilma Derksen	Disappeared	600's	4	96%

Seven weeks later, her daughter's body was found tied up in a shed near home where she had frozen to death. Wilma came home from the police station, and neighbors and friends came over to share their condolences. I think it is really significant that she was being supported by people close to her. Her Mindset Factors had shifted:

		LOC	*AS*	*CS*
Wilma Derksen	Disappeared	600's	4	96%
	Body Found	high 900's	4	96%

Then, something else significant happened. A stranger came to the door late that night when few people were still there. The stranger had lost a child to murder, as well.

The stranger sat in their kitchen and shared the horrific experience of the three trials and his huge absorption with getting justice. He talked of his anger with the justice system and their inability to pin the crime on anybody. He talked about his life had been destroyed and how he couldn't work anymore. He talked about all the meds he was on. He wanted them to know what lay ahead of them. He said it as if it were inevitable. Later, Wilma said that he had forced them to consider whether there was another option.

I believe this had a huge effect on Wilma and her husband, and it directly impacted their Mindset Factors. After the funeral the next day, Wilma Derksen's Mindset Factors were:

		LOC	*AS*	*CS*
Wilma Derksen	Disappeared	600's	4	96%
	Body Found	high 900's	4	96%
	After Funeral	high 900's	<0.5	100

Coming from this totally different place, primarily with the dramatic downward shift in anger, almost to zero, Wilma made the following statement.

"Our main concern was to find Candace. We've found her. I can't say at this point I forgive this person. We have all done something dreadful in our lives, or have felt the urge to."

Through the specific personal support she had received from friends, neighbors and a stranger, her anger had somehow cleared, and Wilma had taken her personal power back. It wasn't until 22 years later that Mark Grant was charged with her murder and in 2011, after a five week trial, sentenced to 25 years without parole. Wilma and her family stayed in their peace through it all and now Wilma spreads the word on the power and peace of forgiveness at theforgivenessproject.com.

What made the difference? Why did one parent go for the jugular for justice and the other live in peace? Mike, Wilma's *and all our human behaviors are significantly determined by a combination of level of consciousness, where we are on the anger scale, and our level of caring for others.* And we show this in our personal and professional interactions every day.

Dr. Paolo Macchiarini - Modern Day High Performer, World Changer

I'd like to share a brief story about a modern day hero and his Mindset Factors. Dr. Paolo Macchiarini, a thoracic surgeon who is doing breakthrough research in Sweden growing trachea from stem cells and saving lives in the process, was featured recently on the CBS television show 60 Minutes. The work he is doing and the lives he is saving is impressive, but it is something he said that really got my attention.

When he was approached by another doctor about the possibility of helping an infant from Korea who was born without a trachea and couldn't breathe without a tube stuck down her throat and into her lungs, he said something like this (paraphrase), "Of course I will help her. She should be dead, yet she isn't. She is crying out for help. How could I not help her." He said this, then acted immediately even though he knew her parents could not afford to pay him.

They shared story after story like this about Dr. Macchiarini. And he kept helping, even as he faced much opposition from his peers and organizations like the U.S. Federal Drug Administration. I knew he was different, and his Mindset Factors show it:

	LOC	*AS*	*CS*
Dr. Macchiarini	high 800s	<0.5	100%

This modern medical hero was already well above the awakened level of consciousness of 600 when he was born and has grown much further. Like above, his behaviors are consistent with his Mindset Factors.

How do the 3 Mindset Factors show up in Facebook?

Let's bring this home to an everyday way we show up and impact the world – Facebook and social media. I saw this exchange on Facebook while writing this book:

Can you relate to these two very different people?

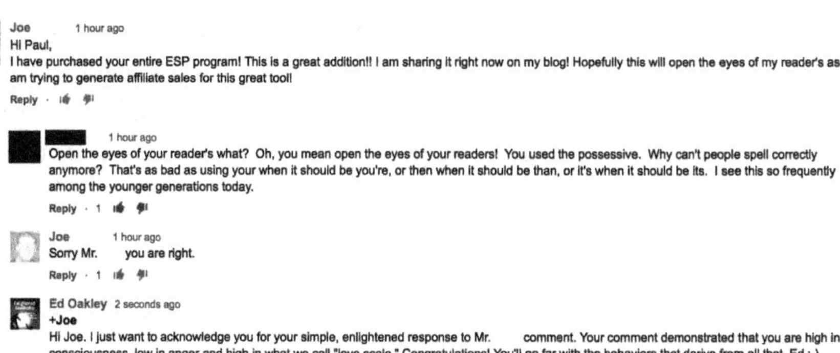

Let's analyze the Mindset Factors of the two people involved in this interchange:

	LOC	*AS*	*CS*
Terry	595	5	74%

Notice how Terry criticizes Joe. Just out of the blue, lambasts him for a grammar error. That's behavior driven by low Level of Consciousness, high anger and low caring for others.

	LOC	*AS*	*CS*
Joe	730	2	94

Notice Joe's polite response to Terry's criticism. That's behavior driven by high consciousness, low anger and high caring for others. With someone coming from a different place than Joe, this could have easily blown up. Which would you rather have as a leader on your team?

Before recently, we would have said that Joe's response was a matter of hundreds of hours of leadership training and personal development seminars. For the last 27+ years at Enlightened Leadership Solutions, we have been putting on these seminars and teaching these skills ourselves with phenomenal results. But what if you could actually BE the person that responds like this…from your very being, rather than managed or learned response? That's what the leaders from these lists are doing and that's the result of our proven 4 step process with Life's New Game.

The secret is that ALL the Mindset Factors are important in looking at leadership and performance in life. It's not just Consciousness Level. It's not just our amount of Anger. And it's not just where we are on the Caring Scale. All three together are important. They are each key components to the formula that take us to new levels of influence and effectiveness.

Are you overwhelmed yet?

Like we said before, it used to take a lifetime of study, self-reflection and action to achieve such levels in any one of these areas, but do not despair! Help is here! In Life's New Game, we've uncovered the proven process that can help you achieve these levels in a few quick weeks in which you have very little to do personally!

Now let's take a look at the 5 elements that pull all the factors together so you can become the leader you always wanted to be.

> *"When we talked about consciousness numbers, just the conversation itself is causing me to see and hold myself at a higher level of responsibility to consciousness. I proceeded through that day with a feeling of responsibility and continued operating at a high consciousness."* Peter

8

THE 5 ELEMENTS TO BREAKOUT SUCCESS IN LIFE & BUSINESS

Writing this part of the book was quite a challenge. You see, there are 5 elements to BreakOut Success and each are crucial to your growth. But what's amazing and encouraging is that *our process to activate* these elements has only 3 Steps!

First, in this short chapter, we'll take a quick look at what the 5 elements are. Then we'll dive in depth into each element so that you understand exactly what we mean by them in Life's New Game. The overall concepts should be familiar.

What makes Life's New Game unique is our slightly different viewpoint on these elements that has allowed us to develop a streamlined process to activate them. It's been a wild ride and we can't wait to share with you what we've learned and how it is already impacting businesses and lives like yours. Let's begin!

When you want to create BreakOut Success, we find that there are 5 elements, that when addressed, will take you to your goal faster, easier and often to an even better goal than you first envisioned.

Everything begins when you:

1. **Decide** for your vision or being. What is it you want to create? Who do you want to be in the world? Every journey needs a destination...even if you end up choosing a different one as you transform on the way.

Next you'll **Transform** yourself in 3 key areas:

2. **Reprogram** your **Limiting Beliefs** so you can grow into your greatest potential… and do it fast!

3. **Clear** for all time your deep, debilitating **Emotions**, as well as **enhancing** empowering emotions, so you can put all your power into the mission you love.

4. **Raise** your **Consciousness** to the levels of all the world-class performers you know in every field so you can turbo charge your action.

Finally it all gets set in motion when you:

5. Take **Action** and step into the person and mission you've created, so that you can put your vision into motion from a place of clarity and high awareness.

Each of these are key, and there are experts who have devoted decades to learning and teaching just one of these elements. Their work has been foundational to our understanding and success. We are going to take a look at each element to get you up to speed on our perspective on each, but fear not! You will not have to spend even one week on each of them to reach your BreakOut Success.

Standing on the shoulders of the giants who went before, our 3 step process will greatly simplify the transformation! But first, you have to know just what you are transforming…

"The main thing I got was clarity. I was very foggy. I had significant energy drainers leeching on me. I am more aware now how to remove them. Clearing so many paradigms and I'm excited and scared about the challenges ahead. It felt so good to have someone have my back. My friends and peers don't have a very high awareness. It can be difficult to discuss this with people who don't understand." Claudia

9

DECIDE

It all begins with a Decision, like the moment you decided to propose.

You'd been dating and trying on a long term relationship and then one moment it just all came together in one crystal clear decision you felt with every fiber of your being – I've decided to spend my life with this person.

Your BreakOut Success begins with the Decision Point, the moment you decide with every fiber of your being, this is what I choose. It's a critically important beginning point and if you don't get this, your success will be limited.

Remember what it felt like when you picked up this book. You were on top of your game, and yet, you knew that there was more to life and your reason for living and making a difference. Or you were sick and tired of being sick and tired you were ready to make a difference in your life and the world. You picked up this book, because you decided this was the time to grow into your next you and you were ready to take that step.

You Decided. Take a moment and lean into that feeling.

That's the feeling of power to change yourself and the world. That's the moment, the feeling the decision point when your total self is in alignment - your conscious, your sub-conscious and yes, even your Higher Self that knows you are here for a reason.

Every part agrees in this moment. You are in your full power. That moment is a Decision Point. And it is from this place of alignment and power that you change not only yourself, but the world.

How can a Decision set things in motion?

That's why there is so much attention on this Decision stage by many leaders in personal and business development. From Vision Boards to acting 'as if' to extensive goal setting. You've likely already read many books on the subject and spent months or years vision boarding and re-vision boarding.

You've been to the Success Training conferences - Tony Robbins, John Maxwell, Jack Canfield or Joel Osteen. And they all have excellent programs and tools so you make some progress. What is key is that when you were at the conference they provoked a decision point and you lock on to the Decision (though many have trouble sustaining the Decision post-conference. That's why this is the first of *five* elements).

You may have felt a decision point when you were looking through a travel magazine and something in a picture captured you and resonates deeply with you. So you cut out the beach with the crystal clear waters and put it on the wall. You don't know yet how you will get there, but you've decided to go take a picture of yourself on that very spot.

A decision point came to Liz when she was living in an area of chemical plants and the release sirens went off for the fourth time that week. She decided she would no longer raise her daughter in that toxic environment. Children are wonderful catalysts for decision points :)

It came to Paula when she decided that loving herself was more important than how much she weighed.

It came to Bob when he looked at his team and knew that if they could just work together, they could finish the project and transform the way their company impacted the world. It was time to lead and he was ready.

You must Decide powerfully in full alignment with your whole self. You've done it before. And with our process, it becomes easier and easier as your essential self becomes clearer.

Here's a few stories of how you may have experienced how making a decision changed the world around you in an instant...

The New Car Bug

If you've ever gotten the new car bug, the moment you realized that's the car you want, you start seeing it everywhere. You wonder how you could have ever missed it before. Once you make a decision, you we see evidence for that decision all around you. It was always there, hiding in the background noise of your life. *Once you decide, you see it emerge from the noise.*

Hiring the Already 'OnBoarded'

One of our corporate clients decided she wanted to hire two new employees who would fit in and enhance the company culture from the beginning. That led her to mention a new employee who was doing outstanding. This woman had already been to several of their client conferences and loved them before she even interviewed. The new person was already aligned with the company culture from day one. So we asked if she could put out a call for those two additional new employees as a discrete part of her next conference. *Her decision to hire to her culture led to a new way of looking at hiring for the entire organization and a much easier onboarding process.*

Remember that the energy is just bouncing around in potential until you Decide what it should look like. The Universe must have a direction to manifest and point to send all the cool stuff to. The Decision point is where what you want starts to take form.

How do Know What I Want?

We've already shared one powerful tool for testing truth - the pendulum, but how do you know what to test?

It's critical you get clear on what you want and your feelings are great guides. Our bodies are wonderful detectors for what we like. They give us incredible feedback for finding our path without our conditioning getting in the way to tell us what we are observing. When we listen to our bodies without judgments, they point the way to our desires.

So what do these guides feel like?

Expansive/Contractive

It's really very simple. When you think about something, do you feel expansive? A feeling like that thing is energizing you and returning energy. Or do you feel contractive? A feeling like you are shut down or losing energy. You want more energy, so spend more time on the people, things, activities that feel expansive.

You'll know it's expansive because you breathe deeper and smile more. Your chest releases and you sit a little straighter.

We had a client who was a manager in her company. She had been unhappy so long, she had forgotten how to dream. We asked her to keep a little notepad on her and every time she had a little expansive feeling, even if it's just breathing a little deeper or having the trace of a smile, she was to write it down.

What she found was what she actually enjoyed doing – even in a job she hated. She hated managing, but she loved teaching the new hires. She moved into corporate training in her company and finally loved going to her work every day.

Paying attention to feelings of expansion help you to decide where you want more of those feelings. But even if it feels good, many people never act because they are not sure that it is right for them. After all, some things, like sugar, feel good but actually can harm you.

You may have been asking yourself:
How do I know this dream is right for me?
Is it worthy of me?
Is it the highest possibility for me?

To get past that indecision, we listen to our bodies to know if we are on the right track!

Imagine stepping inside your dream. Feel it snuggle in around you. See it, feel it, taste it. Just take a moment and let it settle in. Then ask yourself these 5 questions and notice how your body responds.

1. Does it give me life?
    (Did you sit/stand up straighter?)

2. Does it align with my core values?
    (Did you feel yourself center into your heart?)

3. Does it cause me to grow?
    (Did you breathe deeper?)

4. Does it require a power bigger than me?
   (Did you feel yourself reach out for help?)

5. Does it have some good in it for others?
   (Did you just smile?)

Try on your potential Decision and put it to the test. If at the end you feel bigger, more expansive, your whole self snaps into powerful alignment. You've made the Decision, you are sure it is for you greatest, highest good and you are ready to step into that dream.

Another reason people fail to act is because they are afraid their dream *will* change or that they'll get it and not want it.

Warning: as the essential you emerges during this process your dreams likely will change! You will find dreams you've forgotten, or didn't even know you had. It's a wonderful part of the journey.

Does that mean you wasted all that energy on a dream that no longer says *Yes!* to the 5 questions above? No, deciding for those initial dreams and moving on the path towards them is what will reveal your next steps. You may need to grow up a bit before you can even see those dreams.

Decide for what lights you up now, move towards it and be prepared to adjust a little as you grow into what dreams may come.

Now, you may be saying to yourself, "I've had crystal clarity. I've decided with every fiber of my being. I still didn't land that client, assemble the dream team, get my dream vacation or find my soul mate."

That's because the Decision Point is critical, but it's also the first of the five elements. The next 3 elements were not available till recently and if you skip them, you can get knocked off course mid-leap by your old habits and programming.

10

THE 3 ELEMENTS TO TRANSFORMATION

Before you freak out and wonder how in the heck you are supposed to overcome a lifetime of conditioning, baggage and disappointing results, we were given a simple process that greatly streamlines everything that has come before…and it works whether or not people know we are using it on them!

The 3 elements of Transformation are the heart and soul, the power and the uniqueness of Life's New Game. As we mentioned before, the three essential parts of Transformation are:

1. Reprogramming Limiting Beliefs

2. Clearing/Supporting Emotions

3. Raising Consciousness

No longer does it take a lifetime to master one of these elements. We'll show you how you can transform them all concurrently, but first let's look at each of them individually.

11

TRANSFORMATION: LIMITING BELIEFS

Think of beliefs as the little programs or statements we have in our head that we treat as true. The majority of those programs are probably true and useful. Some of them might not be true, yet if we believe them to be true, we respond or react as if they are. Furthermore, like we showed in the previous chapter, beliefs are programs that become self-fulfilling prophecies.

For example, let's take a kind of belief someone might have about themselves, "I'm not good at math."

One of our Enlightened Leadership facilitators, Susan, had exactly that belief throughout school and well into college. And so she wasn't good at math. She struggled with meeting college requirements. That is, until she met a college professor who didn't buy it. He took her under his wing and tutored her. Within a short period of time, she realized she was good at math and actually enjoyed it. From then on, her math grades were excellent!

Let's look at another example, "I hate myself."

Now, admittedly, someone reading this book is not likely to have that extreme belief about yourself, but do think of the implications. Do you see how emotional anchor points would be stored in the body every time there was something that triggered that thought, and the cells involved would be less and less healthy? And do you see how millions of these cells with negative anchor points could eventually cause illness.

Our Life's New Game process includes reprogramming any limiting beliefs that are contributing to the emotional issue. Reprogramming is from negative to positive. "I hate myself" would become "I love myself." "I hate other people" would become "I like/respect other people."

Here is how one of our clients experienced such a switch:

> *"Last week, I was presented daily with a type of person that I did not love. Then all of a sudden, I did love them. I know it sounds simple, but it was simple! I did not love this group of people, I realized it. Then in the next moment, I realized I did love them and it was due to this clearing. It was really quite amazing."* Diane L

Reprogramming Limiting Beliefs

> *"Whether you think you can or you think you can't...*
> *you're right!"*
> Henry Ford

Life is a self-fulfilling prophecy. If we believe we'll never amount to anything, we're right. If we believe we're capable of making a major difference, we're likely to do it! Our beliefs are fundamental to what actually shows up in our lives.

What we believe appears, and while that is wonderful for those positive beliefs we have, the natural process of growing up for 99.9% of us created a lot of negative beliefs – many of which are buried deeply. And we're not even aware of most of them.

That's why people spend years in therapy, digging in their past to find out what they learned that's holding them back. We've done that excavation and we're sure you have too. Not only does it take ages, but there's always those pesky blind spots that hide the very belief that you need to transform the most.

Let's look at a key self-healing approach to reprogramming limiting beliefs you likely have tried to varying degrees of success. We'll give you our perspective and tools to working with beliefs, keeping in mind that the most powerful tool is the process that heals beliefs and emotions at the same time (covered later).

Affirmations

Since at least 1910, when Wallace Wattles wrote his book, *The Science of Getting Rich,* affirmations have been used by many people to try to reprogram limiting beliefs that they can find. This was one of Rhonda Byrne's inspirations for the movie and book, *The Secret.*

It goes like this, if I feel unworthy of prosperity, I might say multiple times daily, "I am totally worthy of prosperity in my life" with the hope of reprogramming what I *really* felt over time. I'd be saying it as if it already happened – with energy and conviction!

Here's the problem, the deepest and most limiting beliefs we have are at the subconscious level. The subconscious mind is many times more powerful than the conscious mind and much harder to reprogram with such tactics. At a conscious level, you're saying, "Yeah,

I'm worthy of prosperity," but at the deep and powerful level of the subconscious mind, it might be saying, "BS! You're not worthy of prosperity! Let me tell you all the reasons you aren't!"

Essentially, you are trying to drown out the subconscious, or just wear it down with constant repetition. While this approach to reprogramming limiting, debilitating beliefs has been attempted by millions of people, the number who have successfully shifted their real thinking is limited. For those for whom it does work, it takes extended amounts of time and repetition. And it does work to some extent. Liz uses a master affirmation for some of her clients as a jump start to get out of a deep rut.

Afformations

Enlightened Leadership has been teaching the power of Effective Questions to leaders for decades, so when I met Noah St. John and read his book, "The Book of Afformations," I knew he had something significant. I immediately began referring clients to his book and concepts.

The concept of Afformations is based on the power of asking questions. When a question is presented to our mind, it immediately starts looking for the answer. You can't ask a question without your mind starting to look for an answer. It is a very, very powerful tool. For example, a leader might ask the team, "What ideas do you have for encouraging repeat customers?" Immediately, everyone starts processing a question to bring their unique perspective towards the same goal. The answers might not come instantly, but they will come!

The key is asking the *right* question. Ask a sloppy question, get a sloppy answer. We find that a very non-productive question to ask a team is, "How did this problem happen?" Everyone shifts into a defensive, protective posture, being careful to not get blamed for the issue. Meanwhile, the problem isn't getting solved. Is that really where we want our team's focus, or do we want to solve the problem? A better question might be, "What can we do to get X result next time?" or, "What can we do now to solve the problem?"

Afformations takes the concept of reprogramming our beliefs through language (like affirmations), but uses the mechanism of questions to invite our subconscious to the team and work with us to a common solution. While statements invite the subconscious to label them 'true' or 'false,' questions send the entire mind on a quest for an optimal answer.

The key to Afformations is Effective Questions, asking the right question – the question you want your whole mind working to solve.

In the affirmation example, we realized that we felt unworthy of prosperity. Using Afformations, to start reprogramming that limiting mindset or belief, we want to ask a different kind of question like, What are the reasons I deserve to be prosperous? Why am I achieving more and more prosperity?

As your mind starts processing these kinds of questions, it starts seeing more and more special things you are or do that, indeed, do deserve prosperity. The more answers you get to that question, the more you feel you are worthy of prosperity. Your unconscious decision over times starts to shift to the positive side of the equation. And because self-fulfilling prophecy is alive and well, your new beliefs start to kick in, your actions shift to those that create prosperity and you become more and more prosperous.

One additional question that is much more powerful than What or Why is the question the Millionaires ask...Who? Who could help me publish my book? Who could help me make it a New York

Times Best Seller? Who could help my company break into the Brazilian market?

Liz asked the question, "Who could help me find the optimal home school curriculum for my child?" When she started asking Who instead of what, she broadened her vision and started asking people she would not necessarily have thought of asking before...which led her quickly to a curriculum that was so perfect, it was like she had written it herself. And the source of the lead was completely unlikely - executive father of grown children who went to private schools.

We also asked, If we could work with anyone, who would we like to work with on the marketing of Life's New Game? Soon after we asked that question, the very 3 people that were our dream team, became available to work with us in surprising ways.

Who is the question that the most successful people ask, and we've found it gets us to the answer exponentially faster. Who widens the vision and gets the Universe moving much faster. It's like the Universe is your Google and once you ask the Who, they go out and find the exact person/s you need and then puts you directly in their path in some way.

While Afformations are powerful, they do have some limitations. They also take time to accomplish the reprogramming – weeks, months, or longer - before significant results kick in. In fact, it takes such significant effort, many people bail out of the process before getting results. This lack of discipline results in lack of progress.

Perhaps more significantly, that answer to the question still has to be filtered thru what the subconscious already believes to be true, so you still have to clear the belief somewhat for this to work really effectively.

With the Life's New Game process, you don't actually have to know what the belief is to transform it. You just need to know what outcome you want and our process clears any beliefs that may hinder or slow down that outcome and strengthen the ones that will expedite the answer. Let me explain…

A Whole New Approach to Reprogramming Limiting Beliefs

Limiting beliefs themselves trigger emotional responses. If someone says, "Would you grab that snake and put it in the field across the road?" I will react or respond based on any emotions that come up. If I have a belief that snakes are scary and dangerous, even if this particular snake is not poisonous, it will likely trigger a "fear" response. Notice the emotion is dependent upon a belief I hold. If I'm a member of a snake handling sect, then I see picking up and moving that snake as a path to Heaven. Notice the totally different emotional response to the same snake.

Being aware that I fear snakes, I utilize my ability to clear the emotion to get that fear down close to zero. So, the fear is now not an issue. But if my belief is that snakes are scary and dangerous, it is going to re-trigger that emotion again in the future. So, it is important to remove or reprogram the belief in order for the emotion to stay cleared.

We discovered the need to reprogram beliefs when the emotions we were clearing for a client kept coming back after being cleared. Once we realized the likely connection between belief and emotion, we tested to see if we could clear, or reprogram the underlying belief. We quickly realized we could, so we started doing that as part of the emotional clearing process. The emotion for that client and for an entire group we cleared at once, stayed clear - even months later.

Knowing how popular affirmations have been for years, we did a little experiment. We found a number of books with list after list of affirmations. One book alone had 200 of them considered helpful for unleashing the natural, but hidden power of people. Since our process is easy to implement, we reviewed all 200 to verify that everyone would want them as part of their belief system. Once establishing they did, we "rewired" all 24 of our Life's New Game inaugural course's participants to remove their limiting beliefs underlying those affirmations.

Not only did they clear in a few hours, they never came back!

I Believe to Death!

Liz and I had been video conferencing for several nights in a row on Life's New Game. The first couple of nights was pretty late, so I didn't think much of her energy being quite low. But the third night, it was much earlier, and her energy was still quite low.

This stimulated me to do a relative measurement of her energy. I measured her at about 40% energy and was in shock. I knew my own energy after a long day would tends to drop down to around 85% if I was really tired. What would it be like to have my energy drop to 40%, I wondered. (Liz says it feels like never waking up would be a relief. Shocking!)

That energy comparison actually frightened me a bit, so I brought it up with Liz. In the conversation, she had a bit of a revelation. A close relative had always told her how important it was to protect her energy, because "during the day, you use up your energy, and you can only replenish it by sleeping. So, be careful how you use your energy. You only have so much," they said. I was shocked at her realization, as was she. We both realized that belief left no opportunity to regain energy through exercise, talking with a friend, winding down with crochet, etc. We knew we needed to immediately clear that limiting belief, so we went through our process right then. The very next night, both Liz and I realized her energy was much, much stronger that it been the last few nights. Measuring it showed 90%, even though it was quite late, and she had had a very full day. The profound impact that limiting belief had on her was scary clear.

Could Liz have used affirmations, afformations, journaling, counseling, etc. to reprogram or remove the belief? Certainly, but those would not have returned her energy by the following night! And the amount of time and discipline required would have been immense. Can you see why we are so excited to share our process with you? It has not only transformed our lives, but those of our clients too.

Now that we've looked at the critical roles decisions and beliefs play in our success, we'll explore one of the most visible, flashy, painful, funny, joyful, despairing elements...Emotions!

> *"It's weird. It's like I can't even describe the things I felt before because they are all gone. I mean, I couldn't eat, couldn't sleep over this issue. Then, later, I would check in to see if it was there. Sometimes a little bit would be there, but as a little time went on, it completely transformed."* Ev

12

TRANSFORMATION: EMOTIONS

*"It's not time that kills us, it's the baggage
we haul through time."*
Jim Strole, People Unlimited

We all have baggage. This part of the process is about "lightening the load" by actually removing that baggage and the key is in clearing debilitating emotions. These 'negative' emotions weigh us down and make it hard to move forward. They create a fog that obscures the truth of who we are and what our real capabilities are – hence the term debilitating.

Even if our consciousness is high, high levels of anger and other emotions hold us back from being who we could be. As we've already demonstrated, optimizing who we are includes all three – lowering anger, optimizing caring, and raising consciousness. Both lowering anger and optimizing caring fall in this element of transforming emotions. Remember that we're using anger as a metaphor or representative of all debilitating emotions, because anger is consistently the biggest single emotional issue. In this work, though, we clear many negative emotions and bolster positive ones.

Top Emotions We Clear

Based on our tests, the following emotions represent 97% of the negative emotions for 80% of the people:

- Anger with Others
- Anger with Self
- Anger with God and the world
- Fears (Failure, Rejection, Future, Death)
- Hurt
- Worry
- Sadness
- Jealousy
- Guilt
- Frustration

All of these debilitating emotions we clear to near zero in Life's New Game groups.

Where is all this emotional baggage stored?

Did you know that our emotional baggage is stored in the cells throughout our bodies. We utilize Dr. Ed Carlson's terminology and call these Anchor Points, or Anchors. They anchor the limiting beliefs, the programming, the emotions into our system – making it worse and worse, more and more fixed as more anchor points are added over time.

Over time, more and more of these limiting belief and emotional anchors are stored in the cells throughout our bodies, creating unhealthy cells. Depending upon the type of emotional issue, they eventually can cause physical issues. Louise Hay's book, "You Can Heal Your Life" is well known for it's cataloging of physical issues and the emotional issues that cause them. So, you could have a physical issue at age 40 that is linked to something that created an initial emotional issue at age 2. Then every time that negative scenario or something similar came up again, another bunch of Anchor Points would embed themselves in more cells of your body, further clogging up your system.

Late last year I found myself unexpectedly in the hospital overnight for some tests. While there, I suddenly found myself overwhelmed with emotion. After a few minutes of processing, it hit me that I was lonely. The feelings were very deep, yet I had not been aware of them. In fact, it was a bit shocking. Once I realized it, I knew I could clear it, and I proceeded to do so.

In the process of clearing, I discovered that ALL the millions of anchor points I had stored in my body around this issue throughout my life were in my *heart*! All of them. I had never experienced all the anchors in one area of the body. They are usually scattered all over. That was shocking.

Do you realize the implication of this? It is highly likely that if I had not had that experience and cleared those millions of anchor points that were all stored in my heart that it would likely have led to heart disease at some point. Healthy cells become unhealthy when these emotional anchor points are stored in them.

That brief hospital stay was a blessing in disguise. I cleared some deep emotional issues that could have led to serious illness at some point. I even had the opportunity to clear some anger for a young surgical resident while I was there. That will make him, part of the next generation of doctors, a better leader and a clearer thinker.

Balancing the Two Sides of the Emotional Transformation

After slogging through all the negative baggage, doom and gloom, the good news is that positive anchor points are also stored, and those enhance or restore our health.

There are often two ways to "lighten the load." Anger is the heavy weight we want to clear or remove. Think of that as just getting us back to zero, though that is quite significant. Love or caring is like the helium-filled balloons that take "lightening the load" to new levels – getting us far above zero. In fact, with enough helium balloons (love/caring) you can overcome any weight of anger. :-)

Our transformation process includes removing the negative emotions and bolstering the positive side of the emotion. That way you are balanced and can put your full power towards your vision, instead of leaking power all over the place in negativity. Once the baggage is gone, you are fully present both to yourself and those around you. The emotions flow through you, without leaving any residue and allow you to experience the fullness of life.

What's this like? One of our clients put it best…

Our friend and a participant in the first Life's New Game course sounded desperate on the phone. I'd never heard him that worried. There was some kind of mistake, and American Express had cancelled his long-term account, which he used for all his business expenses. There were some other complications, and George was a basket case.

The following morning he had a major keynote address to do, and he was in a "world has collapsed around me" frame of mind. He was a bit panicked. "I know you've taught us to clear ourselves," he said, "but right now I just need for you to facilitate it for me. I cannot think straight and don't even know what to clear."

After talking a little more to reassure him and better understand the situation, I hung up and prepared for a major clearing. We cleared fear of failure, anxiety, worry, embarrassment and a few others emotions, as well as clearing his audience for openness. We also got his self-confidence back to 100%. Once this was done, I texted him to let him know it was complete.

The following afternoon, I got a phone call from George letting me know he had "hit a home run" with his speech! "Probably the best keynote I've ever done!," he said. That's a huge statement coming from a recognized world champion of public speaking. In fact, he did so well that he sold $18,000 worth of additional products and services as a result, a record for him. He was ecstatic, grateful and very clear about the value of Life's New Game.

That was fun! It's not very often we get such immediate and measurable results. George, not his real name, is now in the process of creating a speech around this experience.

Top Positive Emotions We Strengthen

Based on our tests, the following emotions represent 98% of the positive emotions for 85% of the people:

- Love of Others
- Love of Self
- Love of God and the world
- Hope
- Joy
- Gratitude
- Forgiveness
- Peace
- Unoffendable

All of these 'positive' emotions we strengthen to near 98% in Life's New Game groups.

Being 100% Unoffendable is the opposite side of anger, according to Dr. Carlson, and it sure makes sense to us. Since Anger represents approximately 85% of our debilitating emotions, becoming 100% unoffendable is an important part of our work. Imagine the value of that one shift!

Let it Flow

In Life's New Game, when we clear the old baggage and enhance its opposite, like clearing anger and increasing caring, we too become porous to life. We feel and experience the same things everyone else feels, but we allow it to flow through us, feeling it and moving on.

Does it hurt like hell when we stub our toe? Of course! But while someone with baggage might say, "Well that's just my bad luck, what a lousy day! Everything is against me!" or "Who put this box here? I knew someone was out to get me!" We say, "ow!," apply a bandage if needed and keep walking.

Everyone has baggage...ready to unload yours and let life and your power flow through you? That's what we are here to help you do.

A Christmas to Remember

A few days before Christmas, I called Dr. Carlson to share the insights and results we'd been having. I had an insight that he could probably do the process, as well, so I shared it with him. Right after Christmas, Ed called me back to share an experience he had.

He described how his son and son-in-law had gotten into a big fight, almost physical, around a little league baseball game in which one was coaching and the other had a son that didn't get to play. Ed was concerned about the threat from both of them that they wouldn't be coming to Christmas dinner.

Remembering our conversation, he quietly began to set up the process I had described to clear anger between the two. He hoped it would work.

Both showed up at his house for Christmas Day celebration and to Dr. Carlson's surprise and delight, one of the guys gave the other a gift. When it was unwrapped, the receiver got up from his chair, went over to the other one and gave him a big bear hug of genuine appreciation. The anger was gone.

I was thrilled to hear this, both for the difference it made in that situation, but also something else. This was the first time we had shared the technology with another and it worked - even when he used it on others! That was the moment we knew we could help others, and Life's New Game as we know it was born - that's a Christmas to remember :)

We've looked at how beliefs and emotions are transformed by our process. Now let's take a look at how we can raise your awareness so that you can see and experience the life, opportunities and success all around you.

13

TRANSFORMATION: CONSCIOUSNESS

Your consciousness mandates how you interact with the world around you. When you consciousness is 'low,' you are only aware of how the things and people around you affect you. A 'low' consciousness has very little connection to the world around them and the only impact they are concerned with is how things are of benefit to them. This would be around 200 on the Hawkins scale we mentioned before. You wouldn't know anyone like this would you?

When you are 'high' consciousness, you are aware of the world and the people around you, not only as they are of impact to you, but as you are of impact to them. 'Higher' consciousness people tend to want to leave the world an even better place than they found it. They also tend to be more caring, happier and more concerned with positive legacy. You wouldn't admire anyone like this would you?

What we've found is that the most highly successful people, who are making the greatest, positive impact on the world are at a higher consciousness. Since our mission is to support and turbo charge world changers, like you if you are reading this, then we also want to raise the consciousness of those we work with.

When consciousness rises, awareness increases, and you start to notice subtleties you never saw before. You begin to notice little things about yourself, as well as others.

If you speak in groups, as we do, you connect with your audience at a much deeper and deeper level as your consciousness rises more and more. You experience how they are relating to your presentation and you adjust "automatically" for greater impact and touch not just their minds, but their hearts.

You might notice that someone you know is struggling a bit, and you'll empathize better – having a greater sense of what they're feeling and why. Better awareness and understanding leads to better communication – the single greatest issue in nearly every organization we've worked with over the last 27 years.

Here is what Diane, a professional speaker and one of our first Life's New Game graduates, had to say:

> *"I just had an amazing two days. Even after only three hours of sleep the night before, I gave the best speech of my career. Not because it was perfect, but because I connected in an amazing way. No panes of glass. Thank you."*

The panes of glass to which she referred are essentially an energetic protection we tend to put up between ourselves and others. People are afraid to feel and experience emotions and therefore put up this barrier for protection. You've noticed it when you are speaking to someone and it feels like there is a barrier between you and you feel like you just can't touch the real person. In this case, Diane's consciousness had been raised, and panes of glass had been cleared and therefore she was able to interact, energetically from complete porosity.

As we discussed earlier, there is a somewhat magical level of consciousness, the 600 level on the 1,000 Map of Consciousness scale, that is considered a breakthrough to the "awakened" state aspired to by Eastern philosophies. That is the breakthrough I had at the retreat. However, that's just the starting point.

When Diane did her "best speech ever," her Level of Consciousness was well over 800. That kind of shift could not have been accomplished when David Hawkins did his research and wrote his book. The worldwide energy shifts that have been occurring in the last few years have made this part of our work possible.

The higher your consciousness, the higher or better your clarity, creativity, awareness, motivation, energy, connection and probably many other qualities we haven't tested yet. So how do you raise your consciousness quickly and easily? We're going to give you four ways, but we consider only two of them practical.

1. Surrender and Ask for Help From God (or your Divine) in a Difficult Situation

The first one is not a choice. It is circumstantial. It always relates to surrender to God, your Higher Self, your Divine (or whoever you honor in that role) in a difficult situation. Here are two examples:

For twenty years, Lyndon B. Johnson, in various positions of power in Washington, had aggressively fought against any attempts to provide equal rights for blacks. He was a known leader in those fights.

On the day President Kennedy was assassinated and the Vice President became President LBJ, my tests show that he experienced a shift to over 600 MOC. President Johnson was a devout Christian and frequently quoted the Bible to illustrate points that he wanted to make. His favorite quotation was from Isaiah 1:18, "Come now, and let us reason together." I believe that Lyndon Baines Johnson, a suddenly shouldered with the world's most powerful position, surrendered in prayer and asked for God help.

The first hint was his extraordinarily humane insistence that Air Force One would not leave for Washington until Mrs. Kennedy was on board, even though he knew she would not leave without her husband's body. So President Johnson, against strong advice, would not let the aircraft leave until both Kennedy's were on board, which was hours later.

A bigger indication of a consciousness shift occurred a few months later when, against the strong recommendation of his advisors, and a 180 degree turnaround on his part, he introduced the Bill for the Equal Rights Amendment. His advisors said it was political suicide, and he simply said, "It is time." Not known as an orator, quite the opposite, President Johnson then proceeded to introduce the Bill with a very impressive and persuasive speech that went far in influencing Congress to pass the Bill.

To bring it closer to home, I witnessed the power of the shift myself recently when dozens of us were hiking up steep terrain to get to a famous cave in Crete. One of our group was a bit overweight and not in shape for such a hike. She fell far behind the rest of the group immediately and had to stop often. I really didn't think she had a prayer of a chance to make it (no pun intended).

We were having lunch near a cave when this same woman came walking up to the group, red-faced, crying – yet with a radiance about her. I sensed she had had a profound experience, and I knew what her LOC had been – below 600. I pulled out my pendulum and quickly determined she had made the leap beyond 600. I asked her the next day and she confirmed that she had given up, surrendered, and asked God for help. In that moment, she had been given

Divine Grace, which is what happens in this shift above the level of awakening. It gave her the strength to not only finish the climb, but to accomplish the feat in love and peace.

These are jumps in consciousness that happen with little warning and no planning. You may have actually experienced something like this in the past, so you know the power of surrender. But, you probably don't want to plan a major struggle so you to have a breakthrough in consciousness, so let's look at some painless ways to raise consciousness.

2. Sit in Meditation Daily

For centuries religions around the world have taught meditation as a way to get closer to the divine. Whether in chant, song or silence, centuries of seekers have engaged in this practice to raise their consciousness. It works. That's why it has been taught for centuries and in many forms worldwide, but the consciousness shifts typically happen over years.

We know personally the power of meditation. Liz picked up Zen meditation when she was bedridden for a year and a half to help her transcend a difficult time. She's also attended a 10 day Vipassana retreat - though none of us can imagine Liz remaining silent for 10 days!

We have many friends, colleagues and clients who teach meditation extremely successfully to enhance the peace both of individuals and corporations. We love and honor them all and attend some of their events.

This is not a book to teach mediation. There are many fine people called to that work and it is worth your time and it will enhance your life, health and peace.

This is a book in which raising your consciousness is a major and essential element, but in the current age, there are much faster and easier ways to raise consciousness. This is a book about faster, easier ways to raise your consciousness.

Liz really struggled with this at first. With a lifetime fascination with mythology and world religion, a Bachelor's Degree in Cultural Anthropology – studying Shaman (or witchdoctors)! and a Master's of Divinity, Liz has spent a lifetime studying and pursuing the divine. Everything she read and learned was embedded with the belief that it took a lifetime of devotion and then maybe you'd raise your consciousness.

How can we possibly say its fast, easy and we can do it for someone – even if they don't know it!

Did you catch the limiting belief? It was embedded everywhere that you had to do it yourself and it would take an entire lifetime (or a few weeks with no food in the wilderness - Buddha and Jesus Christ).

We're not saying that the belief wasn't true before. what we are saying is that we've crossed into a new age - a new game - and in this game, enlightenment has gotten much easier and you don't have to do it alone. We're not the only ones saying this. The next option has raised the consciousness of over a million in the last few years. It just doesn't clear emotions and reprogram limiting beliefs!

3. *Utilize Your Local Oneness University Opportunities*

A few years ago, a husband and wife teaching team noticed that the students in their school were becoming very aware and conscientious. Their families noticed and started dropping by the school to learn more themselves so that they could enjoy the peace they saw in their children. The place became so positive, that the energy literally pulled people into the place as they were walking by building.

That's how the living avatars Sri Amma Bhagavan were discovered and the Oneness University movement began. Not concerned with sects or institutionalized religion, Bhagavan's mission was to spread 'awakening' to the masses with new technology in this age where it could be done faster. And it worked. Millions have passed the 'awakened' threshold of 600 with this hands-on, as well as remote, blessing method.

And, yes, this is the place I attended the retreat in my story in the beginning and Liz and I both are 'Blessing Givers' for awakening consciousness. Most of our work in giving these blessings is done remotely.

If you live in a reasonably populous area anywhere in the world, you might very well discover a group of 'Awakened Blessing Givers' (their terminology) in a local Oneness Movement group. Google them locally or go to the international website, www.OnenessUniversity.org. You'll find a lot of information there.

Receiving Blessings will raise your consciousness, typically a few points at a time if the blessing givers themselves are already above the 600 Level of Consciousness. You will not know who those above 600 are, but its okay because everyone typically takes turns giving Blessings to everyone else in these meetings, so you will get them from all levels, including higher level Awakened blessing givers.

Their meetings are usually very inexpensive, usually for a "love offering," and often occur at someone's home or a church. If you see an ad for a number of Awakened Blessing Givers coming to a big event, consider going and going early. Often, they will be giving Blessings in a separate area before the formal meeting begins.

The only issue is you don't have a way of knowing where you are in your process of raising consciousness. The Oneness University has few people with the gift to measure consciousness and you have to go all the way to India to get a measurement.

Since I was blessed with this gift, I was able to do the measurement for my clients as well as measure how many Blessings they needed for a breakthrough and give the blessings remotely myself. I did this process at the beginning of my work. Even with the expedited tool of the Blessing, it took time and I could only raise one person's consciousness at a time...but that was before Liz and I teamed up on Life's New Game...

4. Utilize Life's New Game™ Process

So what's this new game we keep talking about?

You may have noticed in the last few years that there has been a ton of planetary and universal alignments, solar flares and magnetic shifts in the earth. Just like your body responds to the lunar pull of the tides and the gravitational pull of the earth, all these shifts have had an effect on the electrical and magnetic grids of the earth and our bodies.

In fact, these shifts have increased our sensitivity to energy and made its much easier and faster to expand our awareness/consciousness. That's why Oneness University was able to bring people to past the 600 LOC threshold with simple repeated blessings, rather than decades of sitting in meditation. That's why blessing givers are able to bless remotely.

And that's why our process at Life's New Game allows us in one process to remove limiting beliefs, transform emotions and raise consciousness - and do it for groups and entire companies as well as individuals - whether they know about it or not.

Our Transform step in the process does all this and makes the shifts happen in days or weeks instead of months or decades. We do the raising consciousness part for you remotely and there is a part of the process where you also raise your own consciousness.

You can achieve the breakthrough to above 600 MOC and beyond, along with all the associated benefits without ever leaving home (online), or by coming to a live event.

For our Life's New Game clients, we do daily remote Blessings to get you close to the breakthrough point, the "awakening" point at 600. We start those as soon as our clients register for a Life's New Game course. If you are already past that threshold, which is quite possible since you are here with us now, then we bless you up to the 800 threshold and beyond.

How can we do it? We actually can't. Our gift is the ability to ask your Higher Self if they are ready to raise consciousness (we screen our clients and only work with those who are ready). If your Higher Self agrees, then we simply ask the Divine to step in and raise your consciousness. Your Higher Self and Divine do all the work. Our gift is in facilitating the conversation and the agreements.

There used to be an adjustment time after major shifts, but it all happens quite naturally now. You'll just start to notice more and experience more. It's not unusual to be able to see colors and textures you never noticed before and to smell more keenly after a major shift.

We do weekly group laser coaching to help our clients integrate what is happening into their business or personal life and answer any questions about what they are feeling or the process itself.

Everything unfolds very naturally, but we find that transformation is easier and faster when you walk (or run!) with someone who has been there. We have helped both individuals and businesses to BreakOut success with our process. This is about optimizing your effectiveness and your leadership.

Going into the actual process is outside the scope of this chapter. The point here is that you can awaken quickly and you don't have to do it alone!

Before we go into the actual process, we need to look at the final element that puts all the transformation into motion...

> *"Hi Enlightened Leadership Team! I just wanted to share an interesting indication of change that happened today. I had been kind of overwhelmed by all the "have tos" that I had to get done before Monday morning for work and was kind of resenting the time I was at my computer and not with my two young children, when a really clear thought and calm came over me that said, "I won't work all hours and all night anymore and I will have time for my family." It was a strange thought for me because I'm really not one to say "no" and it wasn't a "complaint" or like "I wish I didn't". It was more like a matter-of-fact statement, not that I wouldn't work, because I was putting my foot down or anything. But more of a calm that what needed to get done WOULD without me working all night and pushing my kids away. That was very peaceful and pointed and I almost didn't realize it happened. Thank You."* H. Burns

14

ACT

"Inspiration without Action is merely Entertainment"
Mary Morrissey

Action itself is the final element and the lynchpin that pulls it all together. You can have the greatest idea or greatest intention in the world, but if you do not take an action towards it, it will never come to fruition.

Duh! you say? In some ways, we agree with you. This book is aimed at leaders who are out to make a transformative difference in the world. Of course you are accustomed to taking action, even massive action. It is still as critical an element as all the others, and easy to miss because it is so obvious to highly successful people and yet can be such a huge hurdle for some.

- When you Decide, you give your imagination and the Universe a direction.
- When you Transform, you are preparing the way for that dream.
- When you Act, you set the whole thing in motion.

The whole process really is that simple.

When you experience a real transformation in beliefs, emotions and consciousness, you will likely know the Action to take. Not only is it likely to be obvious, but you'll be driven to do it automatically. You probably won't even have to think about it. It will be, "Of course!" You'll be highly motivated to do it, and it will be easy!

People tend to overcomplicate the Action element and never get moving. They think that they have to take some massive, world shaking action for their vision to come alive - and you may do that. The first action is usually something really simple…

You ask the question, "Who, if I just happen to meet, could open the doors for my project?"

- First action step: *Brainstorm* a list. You think Richard Branson would be cool.

- Second action step: You realize that you need to be able to express your mission in a nutshell when you meet Richard Branson, so you get Terry Sjodin's book, *Small Message Big Impact*, and start getting really clear on your vision and writing your elevator pitch.

- Third action step: *Ask your associates* to add to your list. Someone notices Branson's name and they have a connection that way. They ask what you are up to and you share your elevator pitch. With a thoughtful look in their eye, they mention a couple other people who would be passionate about your vision.

- Fourth action step: Their belief in your project gives you renewed vigor and you start putting together a business plan and a proposed team. If they did get you next to Branson, you want to be *ready with a plan* to show him you are ready to move immediately.

A few weeks later, you get an email from your friend. They are going to a little party with Branson and they want you to be their plus one. You've got your chance and you are ready.

Did it all start with leaping into Branson's private jet and getting him to sign on a dotted line? It started with a simple question, "Who?" and with the small steps to fulfill the answer to, "If I met my dream contact, what would I need to be ready for their help?"

This is not a case history of a partnership with Sir Richard Branson. It is part of the action process that Liz has used for decades to come to the attention of the top people in her industries, to make an impression and several times, to form partnerships. It's the same process taught by top business and personal development coaches.

It only takes a spark and your action is that match. Take a small step and another and another. The effect compounds until you too are an 'Overnight Success.' In fact, Darren Hardy's book, *The Compound Effect*, pulls apart exactly what small actions highly successful people take for leveraged impact. Liz keeps it on her phone for times when she has run dry of ideas and needs a jump-start.

Once again, entire careers have been built teaching people to take action. You've likely been to an Anthony Robbins conference to light a fire under you more than once. You know the power of action. It's our job here to remind you not to overlook this crucial element.

A side note: Action is expedited in *community*. As leaders, we so often are tempted to be the sole decision maker. When we share our vision and action, things happen considerably faster.

Our work with one training company started with the CEO. She wanted to clear out her baggage so she could push up from the plateau she was experiencing. The company was doing well, but her vision was to 10 times their profit and 100 times their impact by the end of the year. Doable on paper, but she seemed stuck on a plateau.

Like a good leader, she started the journey with herself to make sure she was ready for the growth. I worked with her several months one on one and she made great progress. Then she was ready to take the transformation to her company. We started using the process on her entire company and the culture and communication improved significantly. She even started closing contracts in a month that were more than her record year the previous year. Fantastic!

However, when she took the next step and brought her executive team into the loop on what we were doing and we started working with her inner circle directly, that's when huge impact began and the entire company started to pull together into a close team and share the vision for the company's growth and impact. They started closing their ideal clients and more of them. Their shared action and vision made the difference.

The action she took on her own made a significant difference to her company and to her personal relationships with her family. The action she took with her company and team set in motion her dream for worldwide impact. That's the power of action in community and teamwork.

Our process expedites remotely what dozens of conferences and retreats offsite and on couldn't do.

The process is simple (and we even do it for our clients), but before we go through the steps, we want to take a closer look at how the process impacts leadership and the companies we work with.

> *"Not only has the issue with regards to my good ole mum knowing what I do for a living in future seemingly evaporated, but it appears that our youngest daughter, also now seems to be more comfortable talking about the plans for this book. She asked to see the introduction and much to my surprise, I let her have a look without my blood pressure rocketing up into the universe!!! She then proceeded to proof read it and generally make some really good suggestions, which I have taken her up on. Thanks!"* Edith C

15

LEADERSHIP ON STEROIDS

How does our process impact leadership? You mean other than everything? We suspect it is clear already many ways this affects your leadership ability and your organization, but let's discuss it in some detail so that you don't miss any avenues that may help your business.

Looking at it simply, the more effective you are as a person, the more effective you'll be as a leader. When you've cleared your own debilitating emotions and beliefs, and raised your consciousness, you'll be a much more effective leader.

Management vs Leadership

Management is about control. Positional authority. Pushing. Force. The kind of thing you'd do naturally if coming from anger or other debilitating emotion. With low consciousness, your self-esteem tends to be low. Add high anger to the mix, and you'd more likely come from fear and worry. Your ego would get in the way of your effectiveness. To manage is to control by force - whether it's your diet or people.

Leadership, on the other hand, is about influence. Respect. Relationships. Pulling. This is what you would do naturally if you really care about others and want the best for everyone (within reason). At high consciousness, self-esteem tends to be high and you naturally come from caring/loving and confidence. You have only a healthy ego.

Natural leadership shows up at very high consciousness, low anger, high caring. Some of the characteristics include:

- Forward Focused most of time, on the solution, not the problem.
- Asking a lot of questions instead of giving orders, as that honors people.
- Bringing positive energy and good attitude to work
- Modeling of what you want from others
- Getting results

Life's New Game help leaders unleash the essence of who they already are, so they can show up for success!

Consider Leadership As Energy

Monkey see, monkey do. As an enlightened leader, where your energy is will trickle down to the rest of the organization. You want to maximize creative, productive, positive energy and minimize frustration, anger, conflict, negative energy. Since people so quickly pick up on where YOUR energy is and respond accordingly, you want to demonstrate clear, positive, conscious energy as much as possible.

If you're significantly angry, you're influencing the organization in that direction, too. While occasionally, sharing a bit of authentic anger about something a competitor did that was inappropriate might galvanize your team, in general, anger is not motivating, but debilitating – for you and your team. And it is especially harmful if the anger is directed at the very team you're wanting to motivate.

Anger at others, at self, at God and the world make up an estimated 85% of the debilitating emotions we store in our bodies. When it is there in a major way, it leaks out onto other people, and they feel it. Your words might be perfect, but they will feel the anger and the incongruence the words and emotions. When you're a little high on the Anger Scale and relatively low on the Caring Scale, and your consciousness is below the 600 level of awakening, you tend to be "reactive" – that's the natural and automatic behavior.

However, when you're above the 600 Level of Consciousness, relatively clear of anger and high on the Caring Scale, it will also shows up in the underlying positive vibration to your people. They'll feel honored, appreciated and eager to do what you need done, to please you. You'll tend to be "creative," rather than reactive.

$$<600, AS >= 2, CS < 90\% = \text{REACTIVE tendency}$$
$$\text{vs}$$
$$>600, AS<=1, CS > 90\% = \text{CREATIVE tendency}$$

Notice the only difference in the words "reactive" and "creative" is the letter "c" in the middle of reactive. If you pull that c out and put it up front where it counts, that c might stand for words like conscious, collaborative, creative, compassionate, courageous, caring.

While Anger is the biggest single emotional issue in the way of effective leadership, there are others that create leadership challenges, too, in addition to the consciousness level.

Let's review some of the factors that we clear in LNG and the impact it has on your leadership and that of your people. We'll use the averages of the people in the inaugural Life's New Game course.

Fear of Failure
- average pre-clearing 28%
- average post-clearing 7%

Fear of the Future
- average pre-clearing 29%
- average post-clearing 8%

Let's look at Fear of Failure and Fear of Future together. From a leadership perspective, they are much the same, but they can also compound.

If you're feeling fear about an important project for your business, you're likely also concerned about the future. When these fears are present in significant amounts (like 28% and 29%), the people around you feel your fear. That brings out their fear and stifles their creativity, problem-solving capability and invalidates the "shared" vision for the outcomes. This can quickly become a downward spiral for you all.

Our process transforms all the emotions, including fear, allowing you to stop and actually reverse the downward spiral.

Did you notice in the case study above that the fear doesn't go to zero. Think about it. A little fear is natural in our mortal lives. It is the excess of fear that causes blockage.

Conflict
- average pre-clearing 45%
- average post-clearing 12%

The myriad of conflicts we have going on in our minds is a big issue for leaders. We can easily become overwhelmed with blocked communication and end up on an endless wheel, asking – all at the same time:

- What is the best approach to solve this?
- Can this person accomplish this job?
- How will I deal with this employee issue?
- How can I really decide priorities when everything seems important and urgent?
- How can I find time to deal with this family issue?
- How do I deal with this cash flow issue?
- and round and round

You know what I mean. You experience it every day (and night)!

Once you clear conflict to a reasonable level, your issues don't disappear, but your mind is clear and only what needs addressing NOW shows up. You're not bombarded with everything at once.

Being Judgmental
- average pre-clearing 36%
- average post-clearing 10%

While on the average, some would say that being judgmental is not as big an issue as some others, we find it really important due to the impact it has on those around you.

No matter what you say, if you are being judgmental about someone, they feel it, and it impacts their effectiveness. The feeling of judgment puts them in a funk, causes conflict and psychological suffering in their mind, even fear of the future, and their effectiveness and productivity fall accordingly.

You know what happens next? Because they're even less effective, they feel more judgment from you, and a vicious cycle, a downward spiral is started. This is a lose-lose situation. This is great example of poor leadership in action. I've sure been there – on both sides! I've created the issue, and I've felt it.

Dramatically removing your tendency to be judgmental changes everything. After your shift, you'll still have judgmental thoughts pop up, but the negative energy won't be there. Very quickly you'll reflect on the situation, see the bigger picture better than ever before, and let go the judgment. It is amazing how people respond differently to you once judgment is cleared.

Living Up to an Image
- average pre-clearing 77%
- average post-clearing 20%

Living up to an image is a huge energy sink. We have this image of the perfect leader in our mind, and we're constantly trying to look like and act like that person. By definition, that means we're not being our authentic selves.

Do you think people notice? You bet they do. They notice every little thing we do to show up like our ideal image. Because this happens a lot, they don't even know who we really are. It's hard to respect someone that we don't even know.

The irony is that the key to becoming that best leader we aspire to is to be who we truly are. The real "us" is special. That ideal leader already lives within, once we get all the excess baggage out of the way, and raise our consciousness.

When the transformation occurs, there is a dramatic drop in our desire to be someone else. It opens up the real us, and people begin to understand who we really are. And you know what? They'll like what they see, and they know what to expect. They respond accordingly.

It was a huge shock to me as CEO of Enlightened Leadership years ago when my then COO had a heart to heart talk with me in which he informed me that he and everyone else in the company had a problem. They never knew which of the Ed Oakley's was going to show up for work. They'd rather work with the real Ed every day! Ouch! I hope you cannot relate, but many leaders can :-)

Worry
- average pre-clearing 37%
- average post-clearing 13%

You've probably heard the saying, "Worry is a prayer for what you don't want." There is a lot of truth in that. When you're worried, your focus is on the negative outcome that you don't want to happen. Its a Catch22, because that's where your focus is, and you get more of what you focus on. Furthermore, all the brainpower you use in worrying is unavailable for finding solutions.

But it's not your fault. It's a natural survival mechanism and a deeply ingrained learned response – until you break through to the awakened level of consciousness curve and clear the worry emotion. Then worry will drop off in a major way.

You may still have a worry enter your mind. Very quickly though, match solution to possible outcome, resolving the worry and then it's gone.

Some of our clients wondered if they would lose their edge if they lost their worry. What they found is that the energy redirected to breakthrough solutions, ideas, clarity about what really matters.

A little worry is always present. That's part of the survival mechanism of the human animal. But it no longer consumes your energy and time. Instead it becomes the helpful tool it was meant to be, alerting you to potential issues so you can decide what to do about them.

Living Outside the Present
- average pre-clearing 45%
- average post-clearing 11%

In living outside the present, we're not talking about when you are in an visioning exercise and considering the future. We're talking about a tendency to obsessively go round and round in replaying scenes and issues from the past or the future without constructive learning:

- How did I make that overnight success happen?
- Can I do it again?
- Why did I fail after winning so big?
- Am I doomed to failure?
- What if I can't do it again?
- Have I already peaked and its all downhill from here?
- What if we had done that differently?
- and on and on

All the energy spent thinking about the future or the past is energy not available for dealing with what is happening right now. Some self-analysis is good, so you never go all the way down to zero, but the process does help stop obsessively reliving the past and fearing the future.

Knowing Who You Are
- average pre-clearing 41%
- average post-clearing 98%

Knowing who you are and acting from your authentic self is one shining trait of highly successful people.

We've saved this one for last for several reasons. The average of our high-consciousness experimenters for Knowing Who They Are was only 41% before their shift. This was a pretty self-aware group and that's scary low for leaders of organizations.

When we don't know who we are, we spend a lot of time and energy trying to figure it out, both with our energy and our employees energy. Remember my company didn't know what Ed was going to show up that day? So they had to continually shift their energy to match the Ed that showed up. It kept them on shifting sands, gummed up communication and wasting tons of energy that could have gone into our work.

We start out as kids and know who we are, but then people start to tell us who we are and we start to forget who we always knew ourselves to be. We start making little decisions about how things are and who we are - many of which are limiting. We start piling on these little limiting decisions, and first thing you know, we've confused everything and no longer know the perfection we were when we were born.

With the many layers of decisions and false beliefs, we've forgotten who we are and now spend a huge amount of energy trying to manage all these decisions and beliefs.

Good news! Magic happens when we know who we are.

And I'll let you in on a secret... Who we are is ALWAYS special and unique – certainly at the levels of consciousness for which this book was written.

When we know who we really are, we like what we see. We no longer have a reason to want to change ourselves. We no longer need to create a false image to live up to. We're totally okay just as we are. Can you feel the energy we save by just being us? It feels like a huge weight off to me.

LNG shifts us to high Levels of Consciousness level, while clearing an amazing amount of the layers and layers of B.S., including limiting beliefs and negative emotions we've built up over the years. We are stripped back to a clarity of not only who we are, but the specialness of who we are.

We have very exciting statistics for our inaugural LNG experimenters. After their emotional clearings and consciousness shift, on the average they went to 98% clarity in Knowing Who They Are. That's astounding!

And you know something? When they discovered at such a high degree Who They Really Are, they LIKED what they saw. We feel good about who we are, but not in an egotistical way. We are comfortable in our own skin, and other people feel that. Then they feel comfortable around us. We are confident, but not egotistical.

There is a dramatic increase in Influence Power that frees you up to find new ways to contribute to the health and welfare of your surroundings in a bigger way through your leadership.

We clear many other factors. This was a small sample to show you how much energy and focus gets freed up clearing even this short list of factors. When you make this consciousness shift well above the level of awakening and clear your limiting emotions, you haven't completed a goal as much as you've started a whole new growth curve. It puts you on a path of Enlightened Leadership.

Working With Entire Organizations

Sarah is an entrepreneur and best-selling author who has made a difference with her multi-million corporate training business for two decades, but has always known there is so much more that they could do. She had had some significant people challenges over the last couple of years and when we first started working together, her Mindset Factors were as follow:

	LOC	Anger Scale	Caring Scale
Sarah	599	3	90%

By time she decided to have us experiment with her entire organization, approximately 15 people, her Mindset Factors looked like this:

	LOC	Anger Scale	Caring Scale
Sarah	low 900s	<0.5	100%

Notice how these numbers transformed to the level of the world class leaders we've listed earlier in the book. Considering her extensive experience in leadership roles, and these Mindset Factors, she's now the kind of leader you'd want to work with.

The experiment with her organization was designed to see what happened if we:

- Raise the consciousness gradually of her whole team
- Lower their Anger Scale to virtually zero
- Raise their Caring Scale to close to 100%
- Reprogram a large list of Limiting Beliefs, and any others that might surface
- Clear a substantial list of other debilitating emotions
- Strengthen a substantial list of positive emotions

Because of Sarah's world class leadership knowledge and Mindset Factors, we were already set up for success, but what happened surprised even us. Only two weeks after beginning the team project, I received a call from Sarah. Here's what she had to say:

"I don't know what you're doing, but keep it up! We just had an epic sales month in just the last two days!"

When a team with a shared vision are all at high levels of consciousness and very low debilitating emotions, while coming from a high level of caring and appreciation for each other and their clients, miracles can happen – and indeed, are likely to.

One of the interesting factors associated with the first two experiments with did with entire organizations, both of which had Break-Out Successes, was that most of the team members didn't know what was happening. The work was done "covertly." While that is not ideal, and results could be even better if everyone knew what was happening and were fully involved, it worked very well!

How do we justify shifting consciousness and clearing emotions for people without their knowing it? Simple. We are not doing the work. Their Higher Self is doing the work and wouldn't do it if it was not appropriate for any reason whatsoever. We've had few of those – in which the Higher Self determined that they were not yet ready for the shifts involved. We honor that and we didn't work with them. We screen our clients carefully so that we only work with those ready for massive transformation, like Sarah.

Now that you know the background, testing and effectiveness of the Life's New Game process, it's time to take a sneak peak at the actual process itself. Don't let the simplicity surprise you. Part of its effectiveness is the fast and easy implementation.

16

LIFE'S NEW GAME 3 STEP PROCESS TO BREAKOUT SUCCESS IN LIFE & BUSINESS

If you ever were a student of the Laws of Attraction or saw the movie, The Secret, the Decide and Act elements should be very familiar. What they couldn't tell you is how in the heck do you get clear enough in between those steps for things to move quickly.

They knew that still only 3% were experiencing massive transformation and success. The secret holders themselves had spent decades on the meditation and therapy required for the Transformation elements. How could they tell everyone, "Okay, we're going to tell you the big secret, but its not going to be really effective until you spend half your life getting clear first."

Fortunately, in Life's New Game, the whole process has become attainable for everyone ready to transform - individually or whole organizations can transform simultaneously together.

Let's recap:

3 Mindset Factors

There are 3 Mindset Factors of Highly Successful People and we'll help you bring yours into these ranges so that you can experience your own BreakOut Success. You'll need:

1. **Low Anger** (<2 AS) so you can **communicate clearly** with your team.
2. **High Caring** (95% CS or more) so you can **connect authentically** with those around you.
3. **High Consciousness** (over 700 LOC) so you can **see your path** and those who can help you clearly, including the connection with your Higher Self.

5 Essential Elements

There are 5 essential elements to BreakOut Success and we cover them all in our process:

1. **Decide**, so you can have a **focused direction** for your energy.
2. **Transform Beliefs**, so you can **remove the blocks** that keep you from moving forward.
3. **Transform Emotions**, so you can **clear baggage** and all your energy can focus forward.
4. **Transform Consciousness**, so that you can **see clearly** and **connect authentically**.
5. **Act**, so you can set the Universe's **wheels in motion** and reach out for help.

And now we'll look at the actual process we use to make the transformation happen.

3 Step Process to BreakOut Success in Life & Business

The process is simple and we suggest you track it in a Journal for this purpose:

Decide - Set the intention to get what you desire and write it down.

Your focused desire may transform over time as you transform. We expect that. We also know that your desires will lead you ultimately to your core love, so don't wait. Step into them now. Even if you don't follow that desire to completion, the journey forward always takes you to your greatest, highest good.

Transform - We use this process in a single script that you can download (we occasionally update the script so we are giving you this link to get the latest version. We'll also email you any updates to the process so you don't get left behind):
http://lifesnewgame.com/LNGprocess

- Invite in your Divine Team. Who is your divine team? This is your Higher Self and your personal divine team that helps you on your way. Think of it as your inspiration or your higher power. You want all that power in one place for focused transformation.

- Invite your subconscious to align with your request. It is critical that your subconscious be on board and dead simple to implement.

- Clear your Limiting Beliefs and Emotions, Replace with Beliefs and Emotions that serve your new game going forward. We have a specific script that you will use to tell your divine team what you want to do. Using this clear communication yields exponential results, so please stick to the script.

- Ask to Raise Your Consciousness. Now your divine team can bless you directly, if you ask clearing. Once again, please stick to the script. These words are the triggers for them to know what to do.

- Thank your Divine Team for their help. Gratitude is the vibration that multiplies everything 100 times. It sweeps away fear, welcomes in love and makes everyone, including your divine team and the Universe rush in to help you. When we've gotten tired and left out this step, transformation happened much slower. Thank your team for the turbo route :)

Act - Write down 20 steps you could take to take you into your vision. Circle what feels like the top 3. Do at least 1 of those 3 in the next 24 hours.

Why 20? Because the first ten or so are going to be the same ideas you've always had. They may be good ideas, but we also want the fresh ideas released from your transformation. Writing down 20 allows you to get past what you've already seen into a new perspective. Also, if you do this every time you clear, you will start to see patterns. Perhaps an new idea pops up on the list, but it looks too far out for you. By the time it ends up in your top 3, you'll be adjusted and read to take action.

Dead simple? Yes it is now. The energy and content you've absorbed by reading this book is important to the Life's New Game process. It is unlikely that this will work if you just turn to this page and do the steps without going through the experience of the book first.

When you do this clearing process, you are doing what we do FOR YOU in Life's New Game – communicating with YOUR Divine Team (guides, angels, Higher Self, etc.). They do all the clearing work. Just like when we facilitate clearing for you or your team, we aren't doing anything. We're just facilitating the process that is actually accomplished by your Divine Team.

I can assure you that they are delighted that you are finally asking for this help. They've been waiting for your openness and your request. We also acknowledge where you are and who you are at this time. :-)

Once again, we encourage you to have a journal where you record all your clearings. This will help you greatly in integrating the breakthroughs in your life. The process itself only takes a couple minutes to start, then your divine team takes over till it is complete. Check in at the end of your day to track how much has cleared. Use your pendulum to ask what percent of the issue remains, until it gets down to zero. Depending on the depth of the issue, it may take minutes, hours or days.

As we got the process down and our bodies got used to the clearing, we could transform faster and faster. Then one day it started taking as long as it did in the beginning! What gives! We found that as we improved, our transformation went deeper and deeper. It had slowed down because it was transforming more! It's a good thing we were tracking our work, or we would have thought the process was broken.

Sometimes your divine team is doing all this work, and you won't even notice the change. It's like when you have a toothache and go to the dentist. They fix it and you forget about your teeth. If you didn't have it on your calendar, you wouldn't even notice how much you'd been to the dentist in the past 10 years. Write it all down. You'll thank us later :)

When your Anger with Other clears, you may not notice at first because it is simply gone! If you didn't record your clearing in your Journal, you'd enjoy the fruits of communicating clearly and connecting deeply, but you might forget how it happened and stop using the process. Yes, we've done this ourselves and our clients have done it. We were able to go back in our notes and show them the transformation. Keep good notes and you can enjoy the transformation and stay motivated.

> *"If I hadn't been driving by that old church and reaching for the old emotional pain by habit, I would have never realized it was gone! When we cleared anger with others... it was gone! Forever! I've driven by that church every day for weeks now and now I feel the joy I had in that time there. Does it work, Does it last? The pain is gone and joy remains. It's great to be alive. Thank you!"* Liz

Like Liz and I, you are always pushing the envelope forward, always looking at the next step. Keep a Journal of your journey so that you can look back and see how far you've come. Remembering gives you the fuel to keep going, even when times are challenging. Even if you are not comfortable with using the pendulum yet, keep testing. Use a test partner and the easier muscle testing with the arm outstretched. Even the huge emotional issues are often cleared in a day. Check in so you can record the results and express some gratitude - your Divine Team really does do all the work for you!

As simple as the process is, you may feel overwhelmed. That's natural and that's why we've prepared a solution for you. We want you to transform so you can transform the world. That's our gift and our mission. So let's look at how we can get you and your company down that road to transformation fast!

17

GET STARTED ON YOUR LIFE'S NEW GAME

We are here to transform the world with you. One leader or one organization at a time. We all deserve to live into who we truly are, achieve BreakOut Success and leave our legacy to the world. It takes less work than it ever has to get to that point. We can do it even easier together.

And that's why we've specifically designed the Life's New Game Webcast, that walks you through our very process for achieving BreakOut Success and freedom in life and business.

You've read our entire book. You've seen how this works. And you know that clearing your baggage, "lightening your load," clears your way to faster success and happiness. So if you're a leader who is truly committed to making a lasting impact on the world, you might be wondering how you can implement the process we just showed you for yourself and your team… quickly and easily.

While implementing is simple, we know these concepts are complex. In fact, they are often too complex for print, so we've created a webcast where we'll literally break down the complete process and walk you through implementing it in your life step by step.

In this one session you'll discover a new way to clear your emotions and limiting beliefs and raise your consciousness so you can get out of your own way and on the fast track to success. It's simple and quick to implement and we'll be there every step of the way.

You'll also clarify how to:
- Clear negative Emotions so you can focus your power
- Reprogram your Limiting Beliefs so you can remove the blocks
- Raise Your Consciousness, "turn on the lights," so you can be a world-class leader
- What few, fast action steps, if you take daily will propel you forward fast!

Naturally, if you implement everything we just shared with you, you'll see amazing results in your life and in your business. And that's why you should sign up for the Life's New Game Webcast right now.

When you attend your webcast, we'll not only get you clear on the process, we'll also Raise Your Consciousness FOR YOU, right on the spot.

So if you want to:
- Burst thru that glass ceiling between you and your next level of success
- Get more done in less time and feel energized by your work
- Raise your business' productivity while reducing stress
- Improve authentic communication so your team hears you and responds
- Attain the company culture that your team can't wait to get to Monday morning
- Get your team running smoothly without you
- Leave a lasting Legacy in the world and in your life

Then here's your exclusive link (only for those who've read this book) to Life's New Game Webcast.
http://lifesnewgame.com/LNGexclusive

Liz and I will see you there!

APPENDIX: AWAKENING COMPARISIONS

Awakening With and Without Clearing Emotions/Beliefs

When I went through the infamous retreat, we discussed, and I measured, a number of mindset issues. As I was writing the book, it occurred to me to compare the levels of these issues 17 months later for myself and one other person who has not been through the Life's New Game course, but who was in the consciousness retreat. I will call this person Joe.

Keep in mind what it means that he hasn't participated in Life's New Game:

- he didn't necessarily continue to raise his consciousness further after the retreat
- he has not cleared his emotions and limiting beliefs unless he utilized some other approach
- he has not raised his love/caring scale, again unless he did it somehow else

Joe's pre shift numbers:	Joe from Retreat (no clearing) (only consciousness shift)		Average LNG Participant (general LNG clearing) (includes consciousness shift)	
	April 2013	August 2014	April 2013	August 2014
psychological suffering	85%	46	79	22
fear (average of 4 fears)	29%	19	27	14
fear of failure				
fear of rejection				
fear of the future				
fear of death				
conflict	49%	31	45	19
hurt	34%	24	31	21
dissatisfaction	32%	21	32	19
being judgmental	32%	26	36	17
having attachments	37%	26	51	20
pleasure-seeking	32%	25	35	22
day dreaming	40%	32	41	26
living up to an image	75%	57	77	32
trying to change who we are	68%	48	67	34
worry	42%	32	37	25
mind chatter	54%	35	42	26
boredom & loneliness	21%	21	27	16
feeling of emptiness inside	18%	12	16	9

craving	32%	17	26	13
need for permanence	36%	16	34	13
seeking perfection	48%	27	45	22
living outside the present	47%	29	45	23
Knowing who you are (higher is better here)	46%	65	41	95

Wow. I have a confession to make. As I tested the Average LNG Participant improvement in these emotional/belief factors, I was pleased with some and not at all pleased with others. Then it hit me. We never cleared these specific factors in the Life's New Game course! So, considering that they shifted without directly focusing on the individual issues, I guess I should feel pretty good about them.

But, let's continue our research right her and now. We're going to clear every one of these factors for their ideal value (not necessarily zero or 100%) for our 24 original LNG participants now! Let's see what happens.

After clearing these specific issues to the ideal for each person (Last Column):

Joe's pre shift numbers:	Joe from Retreat		Average LNG Participant	
	April	August	April	August
				AFTER
				Clearing
	2013	2014	2013	2014
specific issue				
psychological suffering	85%	46	79	11
fear (average of 4 fears)	29%	19	27	7
fear of failure				
fear of rejection				
fear of the future				
fear of death				
conflict	49%	31	45	12
hurt	34%	24	31	14
dissatisfaction	32%	21	32	11
being judgmental	32%	26	36	10
having attachments	37%	26	51	12
pleasure-seeking	32%	25	35	10
day dreaming	40%	32	41	13
living up to an image	75%	57	77	20

trying to change who we are	68%	48	67	22
worry	42%	32	37	13
mind chatter	54%	35	42	12
boredom & loneliness	21%	21	27	11
feeling of emptiness inside	18%	12	16	7
craving	32%	17	26	9
need for permanence	36%	16	34	5
seeking perfection	48%	27	45	10
living outside the present	47%	29	45	11
Knowing who you are	46%	65	41	100
(higher is better here)				

Ok, that was interesting. Direct clearing was much more effective than "just" indirect clearing of anger, caring, etc. Note that nothing is zero. What makes sense about that?

For one thing, if you had NO dissatisfaction, conflict, worry, etc., you might not be motivated to do anything. But at some point on the higher end, those emotions are debilitating. If your worry is very high, you might be afraid to do anything out of concern of doing the wrong thing – as an example.

One of the leadership team members at one of our corporate clients had an extreme level of anxiety/worry. It was 85%. That's debilitating! On the personal side of her life, she had been trying for years to become pregnant – to no avail. Through the normal work of our corporate service, we cleared her worry as well as many other emotions, down to 12%, which was tested as ideal for her. Within a few weeks, she was pregnant and thrilled. I cannot say we "get the credit" for that, but when you're consumed with debilitating emotions, physical aspects of our bodies don't tend to work so well. LNG's process frees up your energy from these 'negative' sinks so you can focus it

all on moving forward!

APPENDIX: KINESIOLOGY OF LEADERSHIP

How we use kinesiology to make everyday leadership decisions

Energy Measurement, or kinesiology, has proven to be very powerful in the organizational and leadership decision-making process. If I'm already clear, I just got ahead and make the decision. If I'm feeling ambiguous, I turn to my pendulum for input.

To do the measurements below, I've created a 0 - 100% scale I call Effectiveness Quotient.

The higher the number, the more effective that approach. I'm always looking for 100% EQ.

It works because the subconscious mind is involved in these tests, and the subconscious is far more powerful than the conscious mind. It has access to information we wouldn't know to consider otherwise. It's your gut instinct that's always right and kinesiology lets you question it on demand.

Here's a few ways I use kinesiology in everyday leadership situations:

Making Hiring Decisions

When making hiring decisions for a critical role, it is important to consider all information, including "unseen" data. A corporate client of our LNG work was about to hire for a critical role recently, and they had not asked for our assistance. I realized what they were about to do and asked if I could help. They felt they had been very thorough, but they suggested I do some testing to validate what they had done.

The first thing I did was measure the person's consciousness level, Anger Scale and Caring Scale. The consciousness level was reasonable, so a non issue. The Caring Scale was 85%, which is probably okay, not great. But the Anger Scale was level 5, which was shocking to them. Because of the wonderful comments they had made about this person's attributes and how they showed up in interviews, part of me was wondering if I was missing something. I suggested they come right out, assuming my tests were correct, and ask the person, "I've noticed that you have a pretty high level of anger. How do you manage that so well?"

You could tell they were a little hesitant, but they decided to do it, and the response was very telling. The applicant immediately responded to that question with, "I use the same tools I use to work with autistic children in my current job. Those tools help me manage my anger."

My tests were right. Furthermore, I immediately started to clear the anger of the applicant, since they decided to go ahead and hire her. Her anger is now well below level 1 on the Anger Scale and she is doing great in the company.

Deciding Priorities

Let's say you have 5 important, even critical things to do and just cannot decide which to do first. Define EQ as priority with the highest EQ being the highest priority. Test all five tasks, and you'll get your order.

I always like to create a task called "Other" and include it in the list. If Other shows up as 100%, therefore the highest priority, then I know there is another task I'm not considering, and I better find what it is. If you don't use "other" with this approach, you'll always get a 100% top priority, even if something NOT on the list is more important. So, be sure to use other as a catch-all on any list, so you'll know if you're forgetting something.

Choosing Among Options

There are so many of these decisions that come along, let's just use an example.

The best place to have this meeting, as an example of options, is:

1. in our offices
2. in the clients office
3. at the country club
4. other

I then would use the EQ 0-100% scale to determine the best option. You might have a pretty good sense already of what location is best, and maybe you're just doing this test to validate your decision. Sometimes the most powerful use of this kind of testing is when the answer is NOT what we thought it would be. That forces us to think further about why what the testing said might make more sense. When that happens it also assures us we're not improperly influencing the testing.

I particularly appreciate it those few times it says "other" is best, because that means there are important options I'm not considering.

Liz always says that if you are impaled on the horns of a dilemma, that means there's a third, better option. (Yes, she talks like that! I think its because she's Texan born and bred ;) Considering option you can't see is critical. Adding 'other' to the list allows you to know if there's a better option out there and start asking better questions if there are.

Editing Important Documents

A strategic email or very important report might fit this category. When I think I'm finished with the report, I'll measure it's Effectiveness Quotient. EQ might be 95%, for example, Then I know it can be improved.

I'll then glance at the document to see if there is an obvious area for improvement. If I spot it, I'll measure that area to verify there is an issue. Then I'll fix it and remeasure that particular passage. If it's 100% EQ, I'll check the whole document again. If it's 100%, I'm finished. If it isn't, I'll measure each of the paragraphs or sections to determine one or more of them that is below 100%. When I find one, I fix it. When the whole document measures EQ = 100%, I'm finished.

I've actually done this for friends' published books and they've seen increased response from the edited editions.

Determining If Something is Complete

I was wrapping up this short discussion about Organizational Measurements, and I was trying to determine if I was complete. So I simply tested the Effectiveness Quotient of this writing to determine if it were complete. The answer was 98%, so I knew I wasn't finished. Aha! I can write about "Determining if something is complete." :-) It now tests 100% complete.

Final Warning

Let's be clear that this is a tool, and I wouldn't just do something the measurement said to do unless I could now see why that makes sense, or you have come to trust it because it has been right so often. Don't give up your own responsibility in decision-making even then. Just include this in your consideration. It often forces me to think more thoroughly about the options.

APPENDIX: SUGGESTED READING

Dr. David Hawkins, MD, Ph.D

"Power vs Force: The Hidden Determinants of Human Behavior,"
David R. Hawkins, MD, Ph.D., Hay House, 2002
The author's publishing company has various interesting resources
Go to www.veritaspub.com.

"We can measure Level of Consciousness for you if you like."

Contact Enlightened Leadership Solutions, Inc. if you'd like us to test your Map of Consciousness level. $97, which is applicable to services later if you choose to work with us. Call 1-303-729-0540. We will normally get this back to you within three days.

Get the latest updates and perspectives

Go to http://www.lifesnewgame.com

Dr. John Diamond, MD

http://www.drjohndiamond.com Dr. Diamond's website.
His book is "Your Body Doesn't Lie: Unlock the power of your natural energy." Looks like there's much more than muscle testing there.

Additional muscle testing or kinesiology:

The Perelandra organization, founded by Machaelle Wright, has some resources that will help some people learn to muscle test yourself – without the pendulum. It doesn't work for me, but I'm confident it does for many. Maybe I should try again, as there are definitely advantages of being able to muscle test yourself without having to have a pendulum handy. AND, if you can test via your fingers, you could do that under the table in a meeting. :-)

Description of Perelandra Kinesiology Testing Technique (Self-Testing)
http://budurl.com/selftestdescription

There is also a video version on YouTube:
http://budurl.com/selftestvideo

Using a Pendulum for Kinesiology

The best YouTube video I've been able to find on this topic is by Jonathan Livingstone.

He is a therapist who wrote the book, "The Therapist Within You: A Handbook of Kinesiology Self-Therapy with the Pendulum." The title of the book suggests you're finding your own answers. I just bought the Kindle version of the book, and I think it is helpful.

Here is the YouTube video where he shows how to use a pendulum:
http://budurl.com/pendulum

A few comments I'd make. I grip my pendulum just about 3 inches from the weight so it doesn't take so long to "make up it's mind." :-) I cannot remember, but maybe I started out longer and tightened up the length as I became confident in how the pendulum was responding. I think he's pretty clear, but its important to realize that you need to discover what is "yes" and what is "no" for you and your pendulum. There are different ways they respond for different people. The key is to learn "together" what works for you. For example, my "yes" is an angle to the left between forward-backward and left-right. "No" is an angle to the right between forward-backward and left-right. You just have to figure it out by making statements where you KNOW the answer is yes, or no, and see what the pendulum does.

Core Health & Heart Forgiveness - Dr. Ed Carlson

Core Health & Heart Forgiveness are courses that are quite effective in eliminating limiting beliefs and healing old wounds. They have weekend courses that you can to physically go to, which has the advantage that they supply the people who can do the kinesiology/muscle testing for you – as we can in Life's New Game on-site courses.

What I did required solid ability to do my own muscle testing. If you can do that, these are excellent self study courses. And now I've discovered they have facilitators who can do the testing for you over the phone! Go to: http://corehealth.us/resources/

I personally did the Heart Forgiveness course and both Core Health Series I - IV. It was a huge benefit to me in my healing. These courses include workbooks that give great explanation of the issues and solutions, as well as a workbook section. CDs are included that are used to process your issues. They are excellent.

ABOUT THE AUTHORS

Meet Ed Oakley
CEO, Enlightened Leadership Solutions

Founder of Enlightened Leadership Solutions(ELS) and co-author of "Enlightened Leadership; Getting to the Heart of Change" and other books, Ed has consulted both domestically and internationally in 68 countries over the last 27 years.

His books have over 400,000 in circulation. He specializes in project turn-arounds, change efforts, and breakout initiatives. At least 23 of the Fortune 100 have used, and/or are using his work.
Before forming his own company, Ed was an executive at HP and was noted for starting new roles and demonstrating how to have breakout performance in those roles.

Over the last couple of decades, Ed and his team have created products and services such as Influencing Without Authority for Breakthrough Results, Making Managers into Leaders, Leadership Made Simple…

While these programs were all well-received and created breakout performance by people and organizations, Ed always felt there was more to this "leadership development" thing than they and other top leadership development companies were realizing.

Inspired by a recent personal debilitating illness, Ed has broken the code on a whole new way of developing leadership, one that is easy and gets you closer and closer to who you really are – the leaders that is inside you naturally. He developed a unique and breakout way to optimize the effectiveness of individuals and organizations.

It is highly unique in that most of the work is actually done FOR YOU by the ELS team.

One key point is that this work SUPPORTS whatever "leadership development" work you've already done. It actually is the key to MAKING THAT EXPENSIVE TRAINING WORK! It's the missing piece in leadership development.

Ed currently works with CEOs, organizations and individuals to clear what's holding them back from enjoying the fast track into "Life's New Game: Making the Quantum Leap to Enlightened Leadership in Business and Life." This process is the easiest possible way to get to that breakout level of performance.

Meet Liz Hester
Consultant, Coach, Speaker

This is the hardest bio I've written.

It's easier to tell you about how I served churches for 20 years as a teacher, intern and youth pastor.

It's easier to tell you how upon finding out I wouldn't have a job with my church after maternity leave I turned to internet marketing and became a Launch prodigy, going from knowing nothing to $60,000/mo in 4 months.

It's easier to tell you how I lost it all, but still managed to stay home with my daughter, rebuild, homeschool and build a consulting and coaching business.

All those complex stories are actually easier to recount than the gifts that tie them all together...

You see, I've always been a healer – tho few wanted the touch
I've always known the answers – tho few wanted to hear
I've always reflected your true self – tho few wanted to see
I was lonely being an Old Soul in the Bible Belt.

Ed and I met Nov 2013 and our work took off. Ed has been doing blessings and clearings with clients for some time before we met. I had been doing consulting and coaching. What we found is that my wonderful intuitive way of doing things helps cut thru arbitrary boundaries and make movement happen faster – for those who are ready.

Ask me a question. I'll have the answer or the direction for you to seek it. I always have. That's what made me an effective pastor, youth pastor and teacher. Like a Universal Translator, I'll even put the answer into concepts and terms the receiver can understand. That's why I'm an effective marketer, consultant and coach.

Some of you come from the business world. We'll talk in terms of processes and communication. Some of you prefer the language of math and science and we'll talk Quantum theory, multidimensional theory and tesseracts. Some of you walk in various spiritual planes and we'll talk in terms of Jesus, Enlightenment, Guides, Cosmic Alignments, etc.

We each play our own game. We each play it full out. And together we're all going to the next level. It's an amazing ride. Today we embark on this amazing journey to release all our selves, so we can fully live into this great work we have for this world.

Welcome to Your Adventure in this Life's New Game.

To Contact the Enlightened Leadership Team

Call: 1-303-729-0540 or 1-800-798-9881

Email: contactus@enleadership.com.

(Office hours are generally 9am-5pm Mountain Time.)

Website: **www.lifesnewgame.com** and **www.enleadership.com**

Mailing Address:

Enlightened Leadership Solutions, Inc.

6334 S. Racine Circle, suite 200

Centennial, CO 80111

It's Like a Master Process for Mastering BreakOut Success: ... ALL IN ONE WEBCAST!

Includes online webcast plus workbook and bonus material
$497 value... FREE

The Life's New Game Webcast:
Your 5 Elements to BreakOut Success in Life and Business

This revolutionary process will help you and your organization accomplish any goal, live any dream and become successful in any area they choose. Step-by-step, you will discover proven 5 elements that have helped catapult the world's leading achievers to the pinnacle of their career... and the top of their field.

This is a powerful new process that brings astonishing opportunities and extraordinary results. Plus, *The Life's New Game Webcast* delivers the daily written clearing exercises that help you and your team incorporate this new programming into a compelling new life. Watch as unexplained benefits come your way... important new opportunities manifest...and the world opens its bounty and riches to you— all because you've made the journey through the simple and effective process with the *Life's New Game Webcast*.

Includes online webcast plus workbook and bonuses **$497value...** $FREE

http://lifesnewgame.com/LNGexclusive

Plus, FREE downloadable Vision Planning Guide to insure your success!